GENEALOGY

of the

DAVENPORT FAMILY

and

CONNECTIONS

===

Compiled by

Henry Bedinger Davenport, Jr.

1947

Notice

In many older books, foxing (or discoloration) occurs and, in some instances, print lightens with wear and age. Reprinted books, such as this, often duplicate these flaws, notwithstanding efforts to reduce or eliminate them. The pages of this reprint have been digitally enhanced and, where possible, the flaws eliminated in order to provide clarity of content and a pleasant reading experience.

Genealogy of the Davenport Family and Connections

Originally published by
The Author, Henry Bedinger Davenport, Jr.
1947

Reprinted by:

Janaway Publishing, Inc.
732 Kelsey Ct.
Santa Maria, California 93454
(805) 925-1038
www.janawaygenealogy.com

2015

ISBN: 978-1-59641-357-3

Made in the United States of America

INDEX

INDEX

ERRATA

Page

2   Index, last line, read "Ben" lieu of Bell.

2   Preface, line 6, read "Dauneporte".

22   Tenth line up, read "1925" lieu of 1825.

27   Fifth line up, read "1835" lieu of 1935.

28   Ninth line up, read "1837" lieu of 1937.

31   Third line down, read Jacksonville.

36   Seventh line down, read "Flore" lieu of Flor.

44   Second line down, read "Amelia" lieu of Amelis.

47   Top line read "Placed" lieu of placced.

48   Eighth line up, read "1923" lieu of 1903.

51   Seventh line up, read "Daniel" lieu of Oaniel.

55   Tenth line down, read "1836" lieu of 1936.

55   Twelfth line down, read "Brooke" lieu of Brooks.

67   Seventh line up, read "1734" lieu of 1834.

70   Seventh line up, read "Piatt" lieu of Platt.

79   Eighth line down, read "genealogist".

87   Third line down, read "1843" lieu of 1943.

96   Twelfth line down, strike out "Latter died young."

97   Eleventh line up, read "b" in lieu of m.

Notes Word "down" means from top, and word "up" means from bottom.

PREFACE

"Not to know what took place before one was born is to remain forever a child", says Cicero.

The family of Davenport is an ancient one. Their Court of Arms goes back several centuries.

ARMS OF DAVENPORT

"Argent, a chevron sable between three cross crosslets fitchee of the second".

Crest: "On a wreath a felon's head, couped at the neck proper, haltered Or".

The above crest denotes the office of Magisterial Sergeancy, and is reckoned among the most ancient in England. The Earl of Chester granted by charter the Grand Sergeancy of the forests of Leeks and Macclesfield to Vivian de Davenport between 1209 and 1226.

The genealogy of the Davenport Family in England begins with Ormus de Dauneport, born in 1086 in the County of Chester. The name was changed to Davenporte in the fourth generation by Thomas de Davenporte. Dr. Amzi Benedict Davenport, in his admirable history of the Davenport Family, published in 1851, and revised in 1877, traces the family from Ormus de Dauneport in a direct line down to Rev. John Davenport, of New Haven, founder of Yale College, who migrated to Connecticut in 1637, and laid there the foundation of an Independent State and Church on the shores of America.

Members of the family have held numerous high positions in England, Mayor and Sheriff of Chester, also of Coventry, Member of Parliament, etc., and have even married into the royal family. Margaret Davenport, daughter of Sir John Davenport, of the Ninth generation from Ormus de Deuneport, married Sir John Hyde, Earl of Norbury, from whom descended Edward Hyde, Earl of Clarenden, whose daughter married James II, and was the mother of Queen Mary (consort of William, Prince of Orange) and Queen Anne.

Christopher Davenport, uncle of the Rev. John Davenport, was Mayor of Coventry at the death of Queen Elizabeth, March 24, 1603, and it was he who proclaimed James I. King of England.

The above notes taken from Dr. A. B. Davenport's history of the Davenport family.

—HENRY B. DAVENPORT.

September 6, 1947.

GENEALOGY OF THE DAVENPORT FAMILY
Compiled in the year 1947, by
Henry B. Davenport, C.E., L.L.B., Doc. Eng.,
of Charleston, W. Va.

———

This genealogy is confined to family of Abraham Davenport, Sr., 1714-1789, and his descendants and their connections.

I have in my possession an old paper chart, 11x14 inches in size, made in the year 1757, which gives the names of Abraham Davenport and his wife, Mary Simms Davenport, and their eleven children, with the dates of their birth. At the top it shows that Abraham Davenport was born May 28, 1714, and Mary, his wife, March 25, 1724. The date of their marriage is obliterated, the chart being partly disintegrated by age. The above names are enclosed in a large heart, on either side of which are the pen and ink drawings of two angels in flight. Below, in the center of the chart, is "The Sum of Religion", by Sir Mathew Hale, Lord Chief Justice of England. Forming a border around the middle section of the chart is a row of small circles, six on each side, and which contain the names and dates of birth of their children. One circle is empty. At the bottom of the chart is the representation, or picture, of the Celestial Mansion, festooned with the oak and ivy, symbols of victory, and immediately at the corners are the figures 1-7-5-7, once repeated at the inner corners, being the date when the chart was made. The entries of names and dates of births of children born before May 19, 1757, are in the same handwriting as the body of the chart. Entries of names and dates of birth of children born after 1757 are in a different handwriting.

The names of the children and dates of birth, as shown on the chart, are stated below. The roman numerals before the names are the order of their birth, the eldest having a I, before her name, and so on. The Arabic numbers are given to identify the person; each person named in the line of descent having a number. Thus Abraham Davenport is Number (1), and Mary Simms Davenport is Number (2). Chidren:

I.	Elizabeth,	(3)	b. Feb. 13, 1747
II.	Stephen,	(4)	b. Nov. 24, 1749
III.	Abraham,	(5)	b. Feb. 9, 1752
IV.	John,	(6)	b. Dec. 14, 1753
V.	Marmaduke,	(7)	b. Aug. 25, 1755
VI.	Anthony Simms,	(8)	b. May 19, 1757
VII.	Adrian,	(9)	b. Apr. 9, 1759
VIII.	Mary,	(10)	b. May 23, 1761
IX.	Samuel,	(11)	b. Aug. 3, 1763
X.	Catherine,	(12)	b. Aug. 5, 1765
XI.	Nancy	(13)	b. Sept. 9, 1767

Abraham Davenport (1) 1714-1789.

Was born in England, and migrated to America between 1735 and 1745, and settled in St. Mary's County, Maryland. We do not know in what shire he was born. He married Mary Simms of Prince George County, Maryland, about 1745 or 1746. At the outbreak of the Revolutionary War he was King's Magistrate in St.

Mary's County, and was loyal to his king, until he saw his seven sons march away in a company of patriots, when he called to his wife, saying, "Mary, bring me my rifle, if these d--d sons of ours are going to hell I'm going with them". So he marched away to war at the age of 62 years. Sometime during the Revolution he moved to Berkley County, Virginia, and settled on a farm near Summit Point, now in Jefferson County, West Virginia, where he died in October, 1789, and is buried there by the side of his wife. But the tombstones have been obliterated and the graves can no longer be identified. During his lifetime he accumulated a number of tracts of land. By deed of April 20, 1762, John Higdon and wife deeded to Abraham Davenport, "blacksmith", in consideration of 3,000 pounds of tobacco, a tract of land in Charles County, Md., containing 56 acres, known as Munmoth. Deed recorded there April 20, 1762. He left a will, which was probated October 20, 1789, Will Book 2, page 40, Berkeley County, Virginia, now West Virginia. In this will be disposed of a considerable estate, viz:

To his wife he gave five slaves, and other property;

To his son, Stephen, he gave 200 acres of land, near Warm Springs, being the present Berkeley Springs · he also gave Stephen one slave;

To Abraham, his son, and Elizabeth Conwell, his daughter he gave 400 acres of land on Sleepy Creek; and to Abraham one slave;

To Mary Long, his daughter, one slave and her increase;

To Anthony Simms, one negro girl; to son, John, one negro girl; to his wife, all his household goods, horses, cows, sheep and hogs;

To Adrian one slave, and to Adrian and Samuel, together, 400 acres of land; and to Samuel two slaves; to Catherine Orrick, his daughter, two slaves and their increase; to sons, John and Anthony Simms, 300 acres of land on Back Creek, in Berkeley County. He appointed his wife, Mary and sons Abraham and John, his Executors.

I have in my possession an oil portrait of Abraham Davenport (1), which is an enlargement of a miniature of him made by Charles Wilson Peale, the celebrated artist; the miniature is now in the possession of my cousin, Mrs. Frances Packette Todd, of Washington City and Charles Town, W. Va., who is a lineal descendent of Abraham Davenport. Abraham Davenport was not a blacksmith, as cited in the Higdon deed. At the time he migrated from England none but artisans and mechanics could get passports. The consequence was that many young men, desiring to emigrate, registered as mechanics, carpenters or blacksmiths, in order to be allowed to leave England. At the time of his death he was a large landowner and owned numerous slaves and other property. His portrait shows him to have been a real country gentleman.

Mary Simms Davenport, (2)

She married Abraham Davenport (1) in Maryland about the year 1746. Her emigrant ancestor was Marmaduke Simms (14), who came from England. He was sworn in as Doorkeeper of the Upper House of Maryland in April 1662. He married July __, 1668, Mrs. Fortune Mitford (15), widow of Bulmer Mitford (16), who came from England in 1664. She had two children by her first husband, and four sons by her second husband, Marmaduke Simms (14), who died in 1692. His will was probated Mar. 20, 1692. She died in 1701. Her will was probated Dec. 10, 1701. Note: In the Maryland records the name Simms is variously spelled, as Sims, Semmes, Symes, etc.

Issue of Marmaduke Simms (14) and Fortune Mitford (15), his wife:

  I. Anthony (17), b. 1669; d. 1709; m. (1) Bathia (18) and
    (2) Dusebella ____ (19)
  II. James (20) b. 1670; d. 1727; m. Mary Goodrich Anderson (21), widow.
  III. John (22) b. 1673; m. _____, d. 1723.
  IV. Marmaduke (23) b. 1675; m. Elizabeth Clarkson (24) He d. July 15, 1717.

Fortune Mitford Simms (15) left a will dated May 1, 1699, which was probated Dec. 10, 1701. She devised 838 acres of land to her children. Anthony (17) got 200 acres, residue of said 838 acres.

Anthony (17) lived in St. Mary's County, Md., but migrated to Charles County, where he died.

Issue of Anthony Simms (17) and Bathia (18), his first wife:

1. Anthony (25) b. 169_, d. 1749; will probated
Oct. 14, 1749, Prince George County, Md.
II. Electius (26) b. 169_.
III. Fidelimus (27) b. 169_.
IV. Bathia (28) b. 1700, d. 1737, m. John Higdon
(29)

Issue of Anthony Simms (17) and Dusebella (19), his second wife:

V. Marmaduke Simms (30) b. 1694; d. 1738; will
probated Jan. 17, 1738; m. Mary Higdon
(31). He was born before May 1, 1699, the
date of the will of his grandmother, Fortune
Mitford Simms (15), as he is mentioned in
the will. Also Court order shows he was 16
years old in 1710.

Children mentioned in his will:
(1) Anthony (32)
(2) Marmaduke (33)
(3) James (34)
(4) Jane (35)

Also mentioned in will are ''Cousin'' Ann Cooksey (36)
and Mary Simms (31), his wife, who was made his
Admx.

VI. Mary (37) b. 1703; d. 1738; without issue.
VII. Jane (38) b. 1709; ____; m. George Baxter.

In her last will Fortune Mitford Simms (15) gave to
Marmaduke Simms (30), son of Anthony Simms (17) a
mare colt. Will dated May 1, 1699.

The will of Marmaduke Simms (14) was probated Mar. 20, 1692, in Land Office at Annapolis, Md., Book 6, folio 42. In the will he describes himself as of St. Mary's County, Md. To Anthony (17) he left 200 acres of land in St. Mary's County, and 400 acres in Cecil County, Md. In her will, Fortune Mitford Simms (15) describes herself as of Charles County, Md.

The will of Anthony Simms (17) was probated January 12, 1709. It was dated Aug. 15, 1708.

Issue of Marmaduke Simms (30) and Mary Higdon, (31) his wife:

Anthony Simms (32), b. __, d. 1756. Admr. bond dated Feb. 14, 1756; m. Elizabeth _____ (39). Residence Charles Co., Md. Later removed to Prince George County, Md.

Issue of above marriage:

Mary (2) b. Mar. 25, 1724 (See Davenport chart) d. about 1796. m. Abraham Davenport, Sr. (1) b. May 28, 1714; d. Oct. __, 1789; in Jefferson Co., Va., now W. Va., at Summit Point, and is buried there with his wife, Mary (2).

In her report of the settlement of her Administratrix' account of Anthony Simms (32) Elizabeth (39) his widow, stated that she had paid Abraham Davenport (1) for 9½ barrels of corn due him by her deceased husband. This report further shows, "there are only the widow and one child, named Mary Simms". Report dated Nov. 1, 1756, filed in Prince George County. In the report on the estate of Anthony Simms (32) signed by

Ben Musgrave and James Woods, the inventory amounts to L. 222-18-11½; and at the bottom there is stated,

"Nearest kin"   "Marmaduke Simms"

"Abraham Davenport"

"Nighest kin".

The report was sworn to by the Administratrix.

The Marmaduke mentioned as nearest of kin was evidently the father of Anthony (32), the decedent. Abraham Davenport was, of course, "nearset of kin" as husband of Mary, the sole heir to the state.

ADMINISTRATOR'S ACCOUNT
Prince George Co., Md., Sept. 11, 1748

Elizabeth Simms, Admrx. of Anthony Simms (32)

Son of Marmaduke Simms (30) and Mary Higdon (31) his wife.

Disbursements allowed _____L.137-3-3¼

Bal. to secured creditors_____90-0-0¼

Above balance distributed

   to the Widow, 1/3, of which is_____32-13-6¾

"The residue to Mary Simms, "orphan" of the

   deceased, _____65-7-1½

Land Office, Annapolis, Md. Book 2, p. 94,_____1753-59

Mary was the "orphan" of her father, he being deceased.

Raphael T. Semmes, in his notes on the Simms Family, says, "Anthony and Elizabeth Simms left one daughter, Mary, who, I think, married Abraham Davenport". But in another place he said, "No, she was too young". This remark has thrown a cloud on Mary Simms Davenport's genealogy. There are 30 years between the date of birth of Marmaduke Simms (30) and Mary Simms(2), enough for two generations.

The following facts seem to prove that Mary Simms, daughter of Anthony Simms (32) and Elizabeth (39) his wife, was, in fact, the woman who became the wife of Abraham Davenport:

(1) Anthony Simms (32) at his death owed Abraham Davenport (1) for 9½ barrels of corn. This shows a business connection.

(2) Abraham Davenport (1) is described in the Administratrix's Report as the "nighest of kin". This could only mean a family connection, such as son-in-law of the decedent.

(3) Mary Simms Davenport (2) and her husband, Abraham Davenport (1) named several of their children after the close kin of Mary, viz:

a) They named the first child, Elizabeth, after Mary's mother.

(b) They named a son, Anthony Simms, after Mary's father.

(c) They named another son, Marmaduke, after Mary's grandfather, Marmaduke Simms (30).

(d) They named son John after Mary's relative, John Higdon.

(e) They named their daughter Mary, after Mary Higdon Simms, her grandmother.

Thus, we have the genealogy of Mary Simms Davenport (2) viz:

First generation: Marmaduke Simms (14) and Fortune Medford Simms, (15) his wife.

Second generation: Anthony Simms, (17) and Dusebella (19) his second wife.

Third generation: Marmaduke Simms (30) and Mary Higdon Simms (31) his wife.

Fourth generation: Anthony Simms (32) and Elizabeth _____ (39) his wife.

Their daughter, Mary, (2) became the wife of Abraham Davenport (1). She was of the fifth generation.

Note: The Simms were Romanists of deepest dye. Joseph Milburn Simms, son of James (20) above, had one son and eight daughters. The son became a priest, and seven of the daughters became nuns.

On her deathbed, as related by her grand-daughter, Mrs. Amelia Davenport Strother, Mary Simms Davenport (2) called for her rosary and proceeded to consecrate herself according to the rites of the Catholic Church, after having lived with a protestant, Abraham Davenport, for fifty years, and during all that time being a devout member of the Episcopal Church.

I have thus gone into great detail concerning the genealogy of Mary Simms Davenport (2) on account of the cloud thrown on her genealogy by Raphael T. Semmes. The family to which Mary (2) belonged is the family of the celebrated Confederate Admiral Raphael T. Semmes

The two families were close kin, only the spelling of the names were dissimilar.

Issue of Abraham Davenport (1), and his wife, Mary Simms Davenport (2).

I. Elizabeth (3) eldest child, b. Feb. 13, 1747, d. ____ m. Arthur Conwell May 21, 1781 in Berkeley County, Virginia. She had previously married one Walter Boswell. I have no record of her descendents. If any are discovered they will appear in the appendix.

II. Stephen (4) b. Nov. 24, 1749. m. Ester Violinda. He was a soldier of the Revolution. Removed to Kentucky in 1792, and settled in Clark County, at or near Winchester. Court records at Winchester show the appointment of "Linder" (evidently Violinda) and Abraham Davenport, as Administrators of Stephen Davenport, their father. The date is November, 1802 term of Court. His estate appraised Dec. 22, 1802, totals L. 75-14-10, Crt. Record Bk. 2, p. 31. There is no record of any real estate owned, although his sons, Abraham and Samuel, owned land on "Sulbegrub" Creek in said County.

Issue of Stephen Davenport (4) and Esther Violinda his wife:

(1) Elizabeth b.   d.   m. Thos. Huls Feb. 7, 1795.
(2) Mary Simms, b   m. John Huls Jan. 22, 1800.
(3) Samuel   b.   m. Sally Spillman July 25, 1800.
(4) Abraham, b.   m.   Polly March Jan. 19, 1808.

(5) Marmaduke b. m. Betsy D. Staples, July 8, 1800.

(6) Sally b. 1788 m. Nicholas Merrill Nov. 14, 1808.

(7) Nancy b.   No record of any marriage.

For settlement of Stephen's estate, see Vol. V., page 753, of my old family letters and documents.

Information concerning Stephen Davenport (4) was secured by Mr. Robert Scott Franklin, genealogist, who went to Kentucky at my insistance to look up the record concerning Stephen (4) and Adrian Davenport (9) about three years ago.

III. *Major Abraham Davenport* (5), second son of
    Abraham Davenport (1) and Mary Simms (2), his
    wife.

Born Feb. 9, 1752; d. at Altona Farm, Jefferson Co., Va., now W. Va., April 17, 1825. He was a soldier of the Revolution, being Lieutenant in Col. Moses Rawling's Regiment of Riflemen, Maryland line; also in Company of Capt. Thomas Beall, with his brother, Adrian Davenport. He was commissioned as Major by Governor Lee. of Virginia, May 6, 1793, in the 55th Regiment of Virginia Militia. His will was probated at Charles Town, Va. (now W. Va.) April 25, 1825. He married Frances Williams (40), a near relative of Gen. Otho Williams, at Rockville, Md. in 1788. She was b.   d. Sept. 17, 1829. He was captured by the British at the surrender of Fort Washington Nov. 16, 1776, ad remained a prisoner of war until exchanged 4 years later. In 1793 he purchased of Col. Charles Washington the Altona Estate adjacent to the Town of Charles Town, now owned by the writer, and

lived there until his death in 1825, when it passed to hi
son, Col. Braxton Davenport. He was appointed a Magistrate of Jefferson County in 1801 by Gov. Monroe, of
Virginia. Later on he became Sheriff of that County by
appointment of Gov. James Barbour. His appointment
was dated July 14, 1813. I have this commission. When
he died he left a last will, disposing of a large landed
estate. Forty-eight slaves are mentioned in this will.

Issue of Major Abraham Davenport (5) and France
Williams (40), his wife:

    I. Eleanor (41) b. Dec. 27, 1779; m. Dr. Daniel Ma-
gruder.

    II. Mazie (42) b. Feb. 3, 1782, m. Col. Province Mc-
Cormick.

    III. Amelia (43) b. May 13, 1784, m. Col. Joseph
Strother.

    IV.   Thomas (44) b. Nov. 1786, Served in War 1712;
unmarried.

    V. William (45) b. Aug. 22, 1789; d. unmarried Apr.
19, 1815. He was oppointed Ensign April 30, 1814
in 55th Regiment.
I have the above commissions.

    VI. Braxton (46) b. Dec. 19, 1791; d. Dec. 12, 1862; m.
Elizabeth Bedinger.

    VII. Rebecca (47) b. Apr. 13, 1793; m. James Bryan.

    VIII. Ariet (48) b. Aug. 23, 1795; d. young.

    IX. Juliet (48) b. Oct. 3, 1797; m. Robert G. Jack.
Her daughter, Frances Rebecca Jack, m. Capt.

Thos. J. Manning, of U. S. Navy. She was born Dec. 3, 1818.

Further information of the children and the descendants of Maj. Abraham Davenport (5) will be hereinafter given.

IV. *John Davenport* (6) and his descendents.

John Davenport (6) was the third son of Abraham Davenport (1) and Mary Simms (2), his wife. He was born Dec. 14, 1753 and died _____ 1816. He married Eleanor Harris (50) in 1778. He is buried in Davenport Cemetery, at Summit Point, Jefferson County, W. Va.

Issue of John Davenport (6) and Eleanor Harris (50)
   I. Mary (51) b. 1781; d. 1865; m. John Chenowith 1798—2 children.
   II. Benjamin (52) b. 1783; d. 1831 (known as Col. Ben)
  III. William (53) b. 1785.
   IV. John (Judge John) (54) b. 1788; d. 1855; m. Martha Colston 1808.
   V. Rebecca (55) b. 1790; d. 1832; m. John Blackwell, 1819.
   VI. George (56) b. 1792; d. 1876; m. Louisa Dickinson, 1820.
  VII. Adrian (57) b. 1794; d. 1818; m. Olivia Clark. He was a soldier in the war 1812.
 VIII. Frances (58) b. 1796; d. young.
   IX. Catherine (59) b. 1798; d.   m. Jos. C. Ficklin.
   X. Nancy (60) b. 1801; d.   m. Jno. Randall 1828.
   XI. Eleanor (61) b. 1803; d.   m. Alfred Gaskins.

CRAMER LINE.

I. Col. Benjamin Davenport (52) b. 1783; d. 1831; m. (1) Margaret S. Cramer (62) b. Jan. 6, 1790; d. Oct. 11, 1823; and (2) Elizabeth Smythe (63) widow, sister of his first wife. She was b. April 25, 1795; d. June 9, 1877. Col. Ben Davenport was a soldier in the War of 1812, and took part in the defense of Fort Henry when attacked by the British.

Issue of Col. Ben Davenport (52) and his first wife. Margaret S. Cramer (62).

    I. John (64) m. Catherine Orrick.
   II. Samuel (65) m. Emily Orrick. Lived in Baltimore, Md.
  III. Elizabeth d. 1846, unmarried.
  IV. Ellen (67) b. Feb. 1820; d.   m. John A. Davenport, her cousin, in 1843. He d. 1847 at Woodsfield, Ohio.
    V. Hamilton b.   d. young.

Issue of Col. Ben Davenport (52) and Elizabeth Smythe, (63) his second wife.

    I. Margaret Shannon (68) b. 1829; d. Aug. 11, 1889; m. Nov. 27, 1851, Ambrose W. Cramer (69) b. 1820; d. 1901.

Issue:

    I. Elizabeth (71) b. 1853; d. 1938; m. Rev. J. L. Sherrard. Issue:
Five children, one of whom, a daughter named Elizabeth; m. T. H. Rice, Professor at The Theo-

logical Seminary, at Richmond, Virginia. They had four children.

II. Samuel, b. 1855; d. 1880; unmarried.

III. Benjamin D. (70) b. 1857; d. 1931; m. Kitty L. Spear. They had six children.

IV. Ambrose W., Jr. (72) b. 1859; d. 1928; no issue.

V. Warren (73) b. 1861; d. 1945; m. G. Stevens; no issue.

VI. Eleanor (74) b. 1863; m. Wright Denny; two children:

(1) George H. who m. Elizabeth Herold. They have a son, George, Jr.

(2) Shannon, who m. F. J. Beckwith. They have two sons.

VII. Shannon (75) b. 1866; d. 1927; m. E. L. Morton; They had six children.

VIII. Nannie B. b. 1870; d. 1946; unmarried.

I. John (64) Son of Col. Ben Davenport (52) and Margaret S. Cramer, his first wife, b. Sept. 9, 1809; d.   m. Catherine Orrick Nov. 5, 1834.

Issue:

I. Benjamin, Jr. (77) b.   m. Sister of Chas. Jones.

II. George O. (78) b.   d. unmarried; a distinguished lawyer of Wheeling, W. Va. He was a member of the last (1872) Constitutional Convention of West Virginia. He was on orator of note, a cultivated and agreeable gentleman. He died in his early prime.

III. Catherine; b.   d.   m. Charles Jones, of Zanesville, Ohio.

Issue

Anna,
Charles,
George,
Phillip,
Herman.   Last two were twins.

VII. Adrian Davenport (9), sixth son of Abraham (1) and Mary Simms Davenport (2) was born in Prince George County, Md., April 9, 1759; r. Union City, Ky. died May 2, 1841 (tombstone date) m. (1) **Nutty Chapman** (90) and (2) Ann Ashby (91) widow. He was a soldier of the Revolution. He was on the Pension Rolls of Fayette County, Ky. in 1820; and on Pension Rolls of Union County, Ky., in 1840. In 1812 he gave his wife's (Nutty's) age as 49 years. He m. Ann Ashby, April 4, 1813. She d. 1837. He moved to Kentucky from Berkeley County, Virginia in 1796. He and wife (Nutty) executed a deed in Berkeley County Sept. 26, 1796. Land Book 13, p. 446, Martinsburg, W. Va.

Issue of Adrian Davenport (9) and wife, Nutty Chapman (90) (not according to birth):

(1) Marmaduke (92) b.   d.   m. Margaret Hubbard.
(2) Adrian, Jr. (93) b.   d.   m. Harriet Sibley.
(3) John (94) b.   d.   m. Kitty Higgins.
(4) Alexander (95) b.   d.   m. Eleanor Hopkins.
(5) James (96) b.   d.   Unmarried.

Issue by second wife, Ann Ashby (91).

(6) Barbara Ann (97) b. Feb. 17, 1814; d. Aug. 6, 1899; m. Joel D. **Sugg.**

(7) Abram, Jr. (98) b. July 21, 1816; d. Nov. 15, 1890; m. (1) Margaret Ann Finney (99) and (2) Amanda Grinstead (100) widow.

Issue of Barbara A. Davenport (97) and Joel D. Sugg, her husband:

I. William Webster Sugg (101) b. Dec. 10, 1839; d. Aug. 1886; m. Fanny McCoughtry, b. Apr. 23, 1856; d. Feb. 17, 1885. No record of any children.

II. Ann Dupree Sugg (102) b. Sept. 10, 1841; d. Dec. 1923; m. Gibson T. Waller, b. May 20, 1835; d. Apr. 19, 1891. No record of any children.

III. Amelia Sugg (103) b.   d. 1863.

IV. Joel James Sugg (104) b. Mar. 5, 1846; d. Sept. 30, 1884; m. Union Co., Ky. Camilla Mason.

V. Abraham Briscoe **Sugg** (105) b. **1849;** d. **Nov.** 1883; m. Dec. 1872 Sallie Clements; b. Jan. 31, 1851; d. Aug. 1825.

Issue of Abraham Briscoe Sugg (105) **and Sallie, his** wife:

(1) Barbara Ann (106) b. Mar. 15, 1874; m. Wm. Langly.

(2) George Johnson (107) b. May 5, 1876; **m. Susan M.** Proctor.

(3) Lucy Casey (108) b. Jan. 7, 1878; m. Ben J. **Sparks.**

(4) Joel Dupree (109) b. Jan. 24, 1880.

(5) Aaron Clements (110) b. April 11, 1881; m. Martha Proctor.

(6) Betty Gillum (111) b. Jan. 7, 1883.

VI. John Alonzo Sugg (112) b. Nov. 28, 1853; d. Oct. 28, 1932.

Note: Foregoing information taken from notes supplied to Robert Scott Franklin by Miss Betty Sugg, of Union County, Ky. and forwarded by Miss Barbara E. Conway, of Morgansfield, Ky. The latter is a great-grand-daughter of **Adrian Davenpo** (9) and Ann Ashby (91), his second wife.

VII. Abraham Davenport, Jr. (98), son of **Adrian Davenport** (9) and Ann Ashby (91), his wife, was b. July 21, 1816 in Fayette County, Ky.; d. Nov. 15, 1890 Union County, Ky. m. (1) Margaret Ann Finney (99) Jan. 22, 1845; and (2) Mrs. Amanda Sellers Grinstead (100) widow. She was b. Aug. 31, 1827; d. Nov. 29, 1865.

Issue of first marriage:

I. Abraham Davenport (113) b. 1845; d. 1848.

II. John Adrian Davenport (114) b. 1846; d. 1878; m. Mary Frances Walthen:
Issue of (114) and wife, Mary F. Walthen:

(1) Wm. Frederick b. 1874; d. 1874.

(2) John Abram b. 1876; d. 1894.

III. Thomas James Davenport (115) b. Apr. 1849; d. d. Jan. 22, 1930; m. (1) 1879 Jennie Wall; b. 1852; d. 1879; and (2) in 1883, Kate Givens.
No record of any children.

IV. Barbara Ann Davenport (116) b. Oct. 28, 1851; living at Morgansfield, Ky. in June, 1932; m. Jan. 20,

1870 Union County, Ky., John W. Conway (117) b. d. Dec. 17, 1903.

Issue of above couple, surname Conway:

(1) Thomas Abram (118) b. 1870; m. Katherine N. Robertson Jan. 1, 1895.

(2) John William (119) b. Oct. 16, 1872; m. (1) Mrs. Anne Yeiser; (2) Miss Clemon Lawson.

(3) Berry Leslie (120) b. Nov. 9, 1874; m. Cora Veach.

(4) Margaret Ann (121) b. 1877; m. John McKenny.

(5) Cornelia (122 b. July 26, 1882; m. Oph. McMurray.

(6) Claudia (123) b. July 26, 1882; d. Jan. 1883, twin above.

(7) Hugh (124) b. Sept. 16, 1886; m. Paschal Terrell.

(8) Joseph (125) b. 1889; m. Girtie Hanshaw.

(9) Barbara Ellen (126) b. 1891; unmarried.

(10) Hal B. (127) b. Sept. 9, 1895; d. July, 1913.

(11) Infant son, b. 1897.

V. William Edward Davenport (128) b. July 28, 1854; d. 1855.

VI. Elizabeth Adell Davenport (129) b. 1856; m. James H. Hanks; Children of second marriage to Mrs. Amanda Grinstead.

VII. Mary Paschal (130) b. 1862; d. 1892; m Jas. Joyce. Above information from notes of Miss Barbara E. Conway, of Morgansfield, Ky.

Notes from Family Bible:

Abram Davenport (98) b. July 21, 1816; d. Nov. 15, 1890; m. (1) Margaret Ann Finney, Jan. 22, 1845. She was b. Apr. 14, 1821.

Children of this marriage:

(1) Infant b. 1845; d. 1845.

(2) John Adrian, b. Sept. 27, 1846; m. Mary E. Walthen.

(3) Thomas James, b. Apr. 17, 1849; d. Jan. 22, 1930; m. (1) Jennie Wall Feb. 1879, and (2) Kate Givens.

(4) Barbara Ann, b. Oct. 26, 1851; m. John W. Conway Jan. 20, 1870.

(5) William Edward, b. July 28, 1854; d. May 29, 1855.

(6) Elizabeth Adell b. Apr. 18, 1856; m. Jas. H. Hanks. Abram Davenport (98) m. (2) Mrs. Amanda S. Granstead; b. Aug. 1827; children of this marriage:

(7) Mary Paschal, b. 1862; m. Jas. Joice (or Joyce).

John Adrian Davenport's children:

(1) William Frederick, d. 1874.

(2) John Abram, b. 1876; d. 1894.

Immediate family of Barbara Ann Davenport Conway, see list of children under heading IV. Barbara Ann Davenport (116) above.

Other notes in said old Bible:

Ann Davenport, d. July 11, 1877, aged 63.

Adrian Davenport, Sr. d. May 2, 1841, aged 82.

Wm. Edgar Davenport, d. May 29, 1855.

Margaret Ann Davenport, d. Mar. 9, 1860.

Ann Amanda Davenport, d. Nov. 29, 1865,

John A. Davenport, d. Mar. 22, 1898.

Wm. Fred Davenport, d. Sept. 1, 1879.

Abram Davenport, d. Nov. 15, 1890.

T. J. Davenport, d. Jan. 22, 1930.

Above from notes furnished by Mrs. Barbara Ann Davenport Conway under date of Aug. 2, 1932. She is the daughter of Abram, son of Adrian, Sr., by his second wife, Ann Ashby.

Note: (By the writer, Henry B. Davenport)

In 1932 I found among my papers two letters written by Adrian Davenport (9) to my grandfather, Col. Braxton Davenport. They were dated in 1831 and 1832, respectively, and were sent from Union County, Ky. For a hundred years our branch of the Davenport family had entirely lost track of Stephen (4) and Adrian Davenport (9) and their descendents. I gave capies of these letters to Mr. Robert Scott Franklin, a descendant of Major Henry Bedinger, my great-grandfather, and sent him to Kentucky to learn what he could of the said Stephen and Adrian, and their descendents. He was well rewarded, as a perusal of the notes herein on the families of Stephen and Adrian will amply show.

His full report was typewritten and is bound in Volume 5, of Old Family Letters and Documents, in my library, compiled by me in 1932, and 1933.

In one of Adrian's letters above mentioned, in speaking of two of his sons, said, "Dukey" (Marmaduke) "has been appointed Indian Agent at Rock Island", and that Adrian, Jr. (Dukey's brother) had gone there with him.

The above ends my notes on Adrian Davenport (9), and his descendents.

VI. Anthony Simms Davenport (8) fifth son of **Abraham** Davenport (1) and Mary Simms (2), his wife, b. May 19, 1757; d. June 19, 1835; m. Mary Basil, Mar. 21, 1785, in Berkeley County, Virginia. He was a soldier of the Revolution. Received a pension in Oct. 1832 in Pickaway Co. Ohio. Sold his farm in Berkeley County, Va. in 1793; his wife named "Elizabeth", joined in the deed. Mrs. Flora Alice Davenport Mack, and her daughter, Mrs. R. C. Snyder, entered the Society (D.A.R.) under Anthony Simms Davenport through his son, Basil, who m. Sara Evans; and their son, Anthony Simms Davenport, Jr. married Penelope Ritchart, whose daughter, Flora Alice Davenport, m. John Tallman Mack; and their daughter, Alice Ritchart Mack, m. Reginald C. Snyder, of Norwalk, Ohio. Mr. John T. Mack was a distinguished citizen of Sandusky, Ohio. Anthony Simms Davenport went to Ohio from Berkeley County, Virginia, about 1797, and settled on a 1600 acre tract of land in Pickaway County, received by him for services in the Revolutionary War.

Anthony Simms Davenport (8)

b. May 19, 1757, Piscataway, Md.

d. June 19, 1835, Pickaway County, Ohio.

m. Mar. 21, 1785, Mary Basil in Berkeley Co., Va.

She d. Sept. 15, 1821, Ross Co., Ohio, near Yellow Bud.

Following names and dates from the family Bible of Anthony Simms Davenport (8), viz:

I. Ann Hallam (131) b. Dec. 10, 1780.

II. Willa Miner (132) b. Jan. 14, 1783, m. Morgan.

III. Nancy (133) b.   d.

IV. Joseph (134) b. Jan. 19, 1788, d.

V. Abraham (135) b. Dec. 7, 1791; d.   m. Penelope Griffith.

VI. Wesley (136) b. Dec. 8, 1793, d. Young.

VII. Basil (137) b. June 5, 1796; d. Jan. 13, 1837. m. Sara Evans.

VIII. Ira (138) b. June 1, 1797; d. Nov. 10, 1863, m. 3 times.

IX. Eleanor (139) b. July 21, 1798; d. Sept. 10, 1800.

X. John (140) b. July 21, 1798; d. Sept. 10, 1800. Twins.

XI. Anzelette (141) b. Aug. 1, 1801; d. Dec. 26, 1826, m. Minear.

XII. William (142) b. Sept. 25, 1802; d. 1804.

XIII. Mary (143) b. November 26, 1806; d. March 8, 1877, m. Thompson. Basil (137) above b. June 5, 1796 Berkeley Co., Va. d. Jan. 13, 1937, Ross Co., Ohio, m. Sara Evans (144)

Issue of VII. Basil Davenport (137) and Sara Evans (144), his wife:

(1) Anthony Simms (145) b. Dec. 25, 1823, d. Oct. 17, 1853; m. Jan. 13, 1848 Penelope Ritchart. Residence, Yellow Bud, Ross Co., Ohio. Educated at Kenyon College, Gambier, Ohio.

Children: (1) Flora Alice (146) b Sept. 1, 1849, d.

July 2, 1925, m. John T. Mack (147) Feb. 25, 1873, Newspaper Publisher of Sandusky, Ohio.

Issue of Flora Davenport (146), and John T. Mack her husband, surname Mack:

I. John Davenport (148) b. Feb. 10, 1875, m. Mrs. Blanche Emmick; no issue.

II. Alice Ritchart (149) b. Aug. 27, 1876, m. Reginold C. Snyder,

III. Ethel Beebe (150) b. Sept. 15, 1879, m. Albert C. Blinn.

IV. Egbert Hiram (151) b. June 14, 1881, m. Dorothy Shumaker.

V. Cornelia Penelope (152) b. Jan. 17, 1886, m. Charles J. Stark.

Ethel Beebe Blinn (150) above, had daughter, Ethel Beebe Blinn (153) who m. 1930 Lucius Seiberling, of Akron, Ohio.

Egbert Hiram Mack (151) had two children, viz:

(1) John Tallman Mack (154) and (2) Dorothy Jane Mack (155).

Cornelia Penelope Mack (152) who m. Charles J. Stark, had one daughter, Penelope Mack Stark (156).

II. Alice Ritchart Mack (149) b. Aug. 27, 1876, m. Oct. 20, 1897.

Reginald C. Snyder (157) b. Sept. 25, 1873; Publisher of Norwalk, Ohio, President Associated Ohio Dailies, a newspaper organization.

Issue:

Alice Davenport Snyder (158) b. May 19, 1899, m.

June 28, 1924 Dudley Allen White, of Norwalk, Ohio.

Children:

    I. Alice Mack White (159) b. Sept. 22, 1925.

    II. Dudley Allen White, Jr. (160) b. Apr. 15, 1930.

V. Abraham Davenport (135) son of Anthony Simms (8) and Mary Basil Davenport, his wife, b. Dec. 7, 1791, Berkeley Co., Va. d. Oct. 13, 1837, Shelby Co., Ohio; m. May 17, 1809 Penelope Griffith, b. May 27, 1788. Issue:

Dr. Anthony Simms Davenport (161) b.   m. Henrietta Benham, b. Shelby Co., Ohio. d.

Children of last couple above.

    I. Clementine, b. m. John Mack Hackenton; one child died an infant.

    II. Laura E. b. Apr. 15, 1837, m. John McNaughton.

    III. John Bordrick, b. Aug. 27, 1839; m. Charity A. Runyan, two children, viz: Mary Laura and Richard Beardsley.

    IV. Estelle, b.   d.   m. A. S. Carmen, Oakland, Cal. two children: Clyde Davenport, m. Isabel Taylor; and Ralph W. Carmen, b. Jan. 1875.

Above notes supplied by Mrs. Reginald C. Snyder, of Norwalk, Ohio.

IRA DAVENPORT LINE

VIII. Ira Davenport (138), son of Anthony Simms Davenport (8) and Mary Basil, his wife, b. June 1, 1797, Berkeley Co. Va. d. Nov. 10, 1863, Jaccksonville, Ill. m. (1) ____ and (2) Mrs. Ruark, widow, and (3) Mrs. Reid, widow; mill owner and grain merchant; Sheriff Morgan Co., Ill. Children:

I. David Simms (162) b. 1828, d. 1873, unmarried.

II. Braxton (163) b. 1830, d. 1903, m. Miss Henderson.

III. Basil (Bazzil) (164) b. 1832, d. 1900, m. Mary E. Metcalf.

No children by (2) marriage (Mrs. Ruark)

IV. Elizabeth (165) b. 1840, d. 1912, m. Dr. G. V. Black. Last child (Elizabeth) by (3) marriage (to Mrs. Reid).

Above information by Mr. Ira William Davenport, of Louisville, Ky. (1932)

III. Bazzil Davenport (164), son of Ira Davenport (138) b. 1832, d. 1900, m. Mary E. Metcalf, b. 1842; removed to California 1850; returned to Jacksonville, Ill., 1857; City Assessor, Magistrate.

Issue of Bazzil Davenport (164) and Mary E. Metcalf, his wife:

I. Ira William (166) b. 1863; m. Emily A. Davison.

II. Fred (167) b. 1867; d. 1902; m. Alma Stevens. Graduate R. P. I. Class 1892.

Above information from Mr. Ira William Davenport. (166).

I. Ira William Davenport (166), son of Bazzil Davenport (164) b. 1863, Jacksonville, Ill. m. June 24, 1902, Emily Andrews Davison, dau. Charles E. and Emily A. Davison, b. 1874. Ira William Davenport removed to Louisville, Ky., 1892. Graduated 1885 Illinois College, Jacksonville, Ill. Graduate student Yale University 1887-9. M. A. Yale 1891. Supt. of Public Schools, Jacksonville, Ill. 1889-1891. Graduate student Harvard University 1891-2. Instructor of English, High School, Louisville, Kentucky. Headmaster for Boys, Louisville, 1901-1917. Professor of English, University of Louisville, 1919-28. Retired 1928. Episcopalian. Member following clubs: Pendennis, Arts, Quindecim, Amateur painter.

Children:

I. Basil (168) b. Mar. 7, 1903.

II. John Andrew (169) b. June 4, 1910. Information by Mr. Ira William Davenport, 1932.

NOTE:

Mr. Robert Scott Franklin, who collected much of the information concerning the Simms family, and Kentucky and Ohio Davenports, died at Charleston, W. Va., April 7, 1945, aged about 65 years.

End of notes on Anthony Simms Davenport.

IX. Samuel Davenport (11), son of Abraham Davenport (1) and Mary Simms (2), his wife, b. Aug. 3, 1763; d. Oct. 1829; m. (1) Lucy Cook (2) Mary Hay and (3) Ruth _____. No children. He left will in which he devised 200 acres of land on Fulton Creek to his two nieces, daughters of Major Charles Orrick and Catherine Davenport (12), his wife. He also devised 103 acres of land to his slaves, after having manumitted them and sent them to Ohio. He is buried in Jefferson County, W. Va. In Vol. V., page 327 of my bound notes on Letters and Documents is a memorandum that "Ruth, wife of Samuel Davenport, died Sept. 16, 1823".

X. Catherine Davenport (12), daughter of Abraham Davenport (1) and Mary Simms (2), his wife, b. Aug. 5, 1765; d.   m. Major Charles Orrick, b. 1761, d. Jan. 26, 1833.

George O. Davenport and Benjamin Davenport, of Wheeling, W. Va., were grandsons of Catherine Davenport Orrick (12). George O. Davenport was a distinguished lawyer, and was the youngest member of the Constitutional Convention of West Virginia, held in 1872. See letter of my father, Henry B. Davenport, to Mrs. Collins, Vol. 5, p. 243, of my Letters and Documents.

XI. Nancy Davenport (13), youngest daughter Abraham Davenport and Mary Simms, his wife, b. Sept. 9, 1767. Died in infancy.

V. Marmaduke Davenport (7), son of Abraham Davenport (1) and Mary Simms (2), his wife, was b. Aug. 25, 1755. He was a soldier of the Revolution, and was with General Washington at Valley Forge, where he lost his life. He never married.

VIII. Mary Davenport (10), daughter of Abraham Davenport (1) and Mary Simms (2), his wife, was born May 23, 1761. She died Sept. 9, 1831; she m. James Long. She left a family of children. Mr. John Davenport Long, of Washington, D. C., is one of her descendents. He was at one time Consul to Para, Brazil. He inherited the household furniture of Abraham Davenport (1) and the miniature portrait of him, by Charles Wilson Peal, which I am informed he has presented to Mrs. Frances Packette Todd (a lineal descendent of Abraham Davenport (1).

Issue of Major Abraham Davenport (5) and Frances Williams, his wife.

I. Eleanor (41) b. Dec. 27, 1779; d.   m. Dr. Daniel Magruder.

II. Mazie (42) b. Feb. 3, 1782; d. 1825; m. Col. Province McCormick.

Issue (as per letter of Eula Brock to Miss Zan Gibson, Dec. 10, 1930)

1. Bushrod McCormick, m. Emily _____.

2. Laurena McCormick, m. Marcus McCormick, her cousin.

3. Province McCormick, m. Margaret _____.

4. Brockenbaugh McCormick, m. Louvica _____.

5. Frances Eleanor McCormick, m. James Flore.

6. Mason McCormick, m. Lucy Hare.

7. Thomas McCormick, m. (1) Harriet Hill, (2) Miss Tedfod.

Children of Laurena McCormick and Marcus, her husband:

1. Virginia, m. Capt. Manning, a sea Captain, widower, with two sons, who lived with "Aunt Strother" (Amelia Davenport Strother). Capt. M. died and left her a son, Thomas.

2. Province, m. Had son, Marcus, who, after his mother remarried, ran away from home, and took the name of John McCormick and is now (1930) living in Toledo, Ohio.

Children of Frances Eleanor McCormick, who m. James Flore:

1. John.
2. Anne Rebecca Virginia Flore, m. Alfred L. Knight.
3. Frances Eleanor Flore, m. James Samuel Linn.
4. Julia Flore, m. James A. Cassidy.
5. Fred B. Flore, m. Mollie Samuels.
6. Amelia Strother Flore, m. Edmund T. Phelps.
7. Elizabeth Bedinger Davenport Flore, m. (1) Charles Parker (2) Irvin Brock. Issue, (1) marriage, Fred C. Parker, dec'd and Frank L. Parker—3 children, at Oak Park, Ill. Issue (2) marriage.
    (1) Eula Brock (1909 Arsenal Street, St. Louis, Mo. in 1909) (2) Blanche, 2 children.

Children of Anne Rebecca Virginia Flore, who m. Alfred L. Knight.

(1) Frankie (2) Juanita m. John W. Sanford—2 children.

(3) William Davenport Knight, m. LaRue McCormick, 5 children.

(4) Ethel m. George Shortridge (5) Carrie; (6) James and (7) and (8) Infants, died young.

Children of Frances Eleanor Floe, who m. James S. Linn:

(1) Horace Blanton Linn, m. Catherine Tompkins.

(2) Fred Flore Linn (3) Elizabeth Eleanor Linn, m. James W. Starr.

Issue last couple:

(1) Henrietta Elizabeth Starr.

(2) Frances Flore Starr.

NOTE:

Frances Eleanor Flore, above named, b. 1836, lived at Altona with her great uncle, Braxton Davenport, about eight years, 1845-1853, when she went to Missouri to live with her parents.

Children of Horace Blanton Linn and Catherine Tompkins, his wife:

1. Clifton Marie Linn, m. Thomas Nelson—one child, Linn Thomas. She entered D.A.R. thru Abraham Davenport, Jr., No. 96572-XCXII-178.

2. Homer Davenport Linn, b. 1867, d. 1895.

3. Elizabeth Eleanor Linn, b.   m. James W. Starr

Issue:

(1)Frances Flore Starr.

(2) Henrietta Elizabeth Starr.

Following from two letters from Mrs. John W. Starr, in 1898:

Frances Flore Linn had five sisters and one brother, viz:

(1) "Aunt Bet"—Elizabeth Flore, aged 83, m. (1) Charles Parker (a felo de se') and (2) ____ Brock. Issue of first marriage a son, Frank Linn Parker; and a dau. by second marriage.

(2) Julia Cassidy, had son who called himself Kenneth Davenport. He was an actor, and was private secretary to Doug. Fairbanks.

(3) Anne, m. Dr. Knight; their dau. m. J. W. Sanford; a son, Wm. D. Knight, lives in Carthage, Mo.

(4) Mrs. George Shortridge, of Macon, Mo.

(5) Amelia Strother, who m. Edmund T. Phelps. They had issue:

    (a) Frank F. Phelps, of Cedar Rapids, Ia. He has 2 sons.

(6) Dr. Fred B. Flore, brother of Mrs. Linn, d. at close of Civil War.

Children of Julia Flore, and James A. Cassidy, her husband.

1. Anne Lilly Cassidy, m. Robert Grierson—5 children.
2. James Flore Cassidy, m. Alice Cotter.
3. Eleanor Strother Cassidy.
4. James Powell Cassidy, m. Helen Thorell—one child.
5. Kenneth Davenport (he dropped the Cassidy) Actor; Private Secretary to Douglas Fairbanks; he died 1942.

Children of Amelia Strother Flore and Edmund T. Phelps, her husband.

1. Edmund Lee Phelps, d. 1926.
2. Clarence Phelps.
3. Frank Flore Phelps, m. Faye Leedham Pippins.

Issue: (1) Edmund Strother Phelps, b. 1900, m. 1930 Florence Stone.

(2) Frank L. Phelps, b. 1912.

Residence, Frank Flore Phelps, 1932, 521 Fairview Blvd., Cedar Rapids, Iowa.

Children of Major Abraham Davenport, Continued:

III. Amelia Davenport (43), b. May 13, 1784; m. Col. Joseph Strother May 8, 1808; she d. 1862. They had no children. He was a lawyer, and lived at Charles Town, Va., now W. Va.

IV. Thomas Davenport (44) b. Nov. 19, 1786; soldier in the War of 1812; took part in the defense of Fort McHenry, when attacked by the British, in Sept. 1814. He died unmarried. He was a very tall, large man.

V. William Davenport (45), b. Aug. 22, 1799; d. April 19, 1815, unmarried. He is buried at Charles Town, W. Va., in the Davenport lot, in Edgehill Cemetery.

See p. 16 Ante for his Military Commission.

VI. Braxton Davenport (46) b. Dec. 19, 1791; d. Dec. 12, 1862, at his home, Altona, near Charles Town, W. Va. m. Elizabeth Bedinger, Sept. 1, 1830, dau.

Major Henry Bedinger and Rachel Strode, his wife:

Children:

1. Henry Bedinger Davenport (191) b. Sept. 9, 1831. d. Sept. 15, 1901.

2. Frances Williams Davenport (198) b. Dec. 6, 1834; d. Oct. 21, 1909.

III. John Davenport (54) third son of John Davenport (6) and Eleanor Mary Harris, his wife, was b. 1788; d. 1855; m. Martha Colston 1808; Removed to Ohio about 1815; located at Barnesville, where he established two of his sons, Colston and Benjamin, in business. Later he removed to Woodsfield, Ohio, where he established two other sons, John Adrian and John Harris, in business. He served as a Judge; and was also a Member of the Congress of the U. S. He and his wife had ten children. He was known as Judge John Davenport.

Issue:

I. Colston (170) b. Jeff. Co. Va. 1811; m. Ella Hickman.

II. Ellen (171) b. Feb. 5, 1811; m. Joe Hare; he d. 1883. She went to Astoria, Oregon, and on Feb. 5, 1911 celebrated her 100th Anniversary. See below for children:

III. Benjamin, Jr. (172) b. 1814; d. 1855; m. Anne Marie Bradshaw. Left 10 children.

IV. Mary Anne (173)

V. John Adrian (174)

VI. William (175)

VII. John Harris (176)

VIII. Joseph Allen (177)

IX. Martha (178)

X. Samuel (179)

Children of Ellen Davenport and Joseph Hare, surname Hare:

I. John Richard Hare.

II. William Hare.

III. Flora Jane Hare.

IV. Theopholis Hare.

V. Martha Hare.

VI. Joseph Hare.

VII. Charles Colston Hare.

VIII. Heber Hare.

IX. Robert Hare.

X. Frank Hare.

XI. Rose Hare.

XII. George Hare.

III. Benjamin Davenport, Jr. (172) second son of John Davenport (54) and Martha Colston, his wife, was b. in Jeff. Co. Va. 1814. Came to Barnsville, Ohio with his parents when 4 years old. Engaged in the mercantile business there the most of his life. Served as P. M. and Superintendent of Sunday School. m. Ann Maria Bradshaw (180); moved to St. Clairsville, Ohio; d. 1855; left 10 children, viz:

Children of Benjamin Davenport, Jr. (172) and Ann
Maria Bradshaw, his wife:

    I. Ellen Mary (181) b. 1835; d. 1910.
    II. John William (182) b. 1838; d. 1838.
    III. James Colston (183) b.
    IV. Harriet Frances (184) b. 1843; d. 1929.
    V. Martha Lavinia (185) b.
    VI. Ann Maria (186) b.
    VII. Rebecca Catherine (187) b.   d. 1852.
    VIII. Adriana (188) b.
    IX. Julia (189) b.
    X. Elizabeth (190) b.

In Vol. 1, p. 208, of the bound volumes of my Letters
and Documents is a letter from Col. Benjamin Davenport
(52) to his father, John Davenport (6) dated at Baltimore, Md. Sept. 17, 1814. From this letter it appears
that Benjamin Davenport (52) was in the Military Service of the U. S. in the War of 1812. He mentions "Margaret" (presumably his wife). He tells about the bom-
bardment of Fort McHenry by the British. He says that
Thomas Davenport (44), presumably his cousin, son of
Major Abraham Davenport (5) "is very ill, fits and chills
and fever". He signs letter, "Your dutiful son, Benjamin Davenport." John Davenport (6) was a land surveyor. In 1811 he surveyed a part of Altona Farm for
his brother, Major Abraham Davenport (5) See p. 199,
Vol. 1, my Letters and Documents. In Oct. 1795 John
Davenport (6) consigned L-30-5-3 of tobacco to Joshua
Johnson in London, England. See p. 207, of said Vol. 1.

John Davenport (6) b. Dec. 14, 1753, was a private in Capt. Samuel J. Cabell's Co. 6th Regiment, Lt. Col. Jas. Hedrick, commanding.

Col. Benjamin Davenport (52), eldest son of John Davenport (6) and Eleanor Harris, his wife, was a brother of Congressman John Davenport (54) of Woodsfield, Ohio. Mrs. Collins, wife of Judge J. H. Collins, Chief Counsel of the B. & O. R. R. west of Ohio River about 1895-1900, was a grand-daughter of Congressman John Davenport (54). Mary, a sister of Congressman John Davenport (54) m. Col. Chenoweth, of Berkeley Co., Va. Their son, George Davenport Chenowith m. Miss Crawford of New Jersey. Their son, William Crawford, graduated from West Point. He m. the only daughter of Fernando Wood, the distinguished New Yorker. He is author of a book on the Chenowith and Cromwell families, a copy of which he presented to my brother, Braxton Davenport, now deceased, in 1896.

BRAXTON DAVENPORT LINE.

VI. Col. Braxton Davenport (46), third son of Major Abraham Davenport (5) and Frances William (40), his wife, was born in Berkeley County, Va. (now W. Va.) Dec. 19, 1791; and died at his home, Altona, in Jefferson Co., Va. (Now W. Va.) Dec. 12, 1862. He was educated by private tutors, and at Dickinson College, at Carlisle, Pa. At college he was a class mate and friend of James Buchanan, afterwards President of the United States. He served as Lieutenant and Major in the War of 1812. He was offered a commission in the regular army, but declined the appointment. He served four terms in the Legislature of Virginia, and served for a number of years as Lieutenant Colonel in the 55th Regiment of Virginia Militia.. He was Deputy Sheriff of Jefferson County, and for a number of years the Presiding Magistrate in the County Court of that County; and it was before his Court that John Brown and his confederates were arraigned and remanded to jail. I have his commissions as follows: As Captain, dated June 1, 1814; as Major, dated April 26, 1821; as Lt. Colonel, dated Sept. 13, 1825. He inherited the Altona Estate, of about 600 acres of blue grass land, from his father, Major Abraham Davenport, who died in 1825, and lived thereon until his death in 1862. On Sept. 1, 1830 he married Elizabeth Bedinger, daughter of Major Henry Bedinger, to which union there was born two children, viz:

I. Henry Bedinger Davenport (191) b. Sept. 9, 1831; d. Sept. 15, 1901; m. Martha Irvine Clay (192) b.

Feb. 1, 1832; d. May 28, 1908, dau. of Hon. Brutus J. Clay and Amelis (Field) Clay, his wife. He was educated by private tutors, and at the University of Virginia. He served as Lieutenant in Captain Rowan's Company of Militia at the capture and trial of John Brown, and his associates. He served in the same capacity in Company A. Sec-Regiment of Virginia Militia, in the Confederate Army during the Civil War. After the war he returned to his estate "Altona", and lived thereon until his death in September, 1901.

Issue of Henry B. Davenport (191) and Martha Clay (192), his wife.

(a)   I. Junius Clay Davenport (193) b. Oct. 3, 1860; d. Feb. 1, 1945; m. Mary Trout, dau. of Hon. Henry S. Trout of Roanoke, Va.

Issue:

(1) Junius Clay Davenport, Jr., b. Sept. 8, 1902. On Sept. 3, 1938, m. Virginia Stone Dilger; lives on Long Island, N. Y. Issue: Junius Clay Davenport II.

(2)   Anne Thomas Davenport, b.   m. Oct. 29, 1930, John Franklyn Newson; lives at Roanoke, Va. Mr. Newson is a civil engineer in the employ of the N. & W. R. R.

Issue:

(a) John Franklyn Newsom, Jr. b. Feb. 24, 1936.

(b) Mary Trout, b. Dec. 6, 1938.

(b)   II. Ezekiel Clay Davenport (194) b. Jan. 9, 1864. Educated at Charles Town Academy and the Rens-

selaer Polytechnic Institute, from which he graduated in 1886 with the degree of Civil Engineer. After
his graduation he pursued his avocation as engineer
for a number of years with the N. & W. and B. & O.
Railroads. He retired on account of an injury in
1909, and went to Florida, where he developed a fine
citrus farm. He is unmarried, and is now (1947),
living in Charles Town, W. Va.

(c)   III. Henry B. Davenport, Jr. (195) b. Feb. 11,
1865. Educated at Charles Town Academy; St.
John's College, at Annapolis, Md. and the Rensselaer Polytechnic Institute, from which he graduated
with the degree of Civil Engineer in the class of 1886.
In 1892 he took a Post Graduate Course in differen-
tial and integral calculus and rational Mechanics at
the University of Virginia; was Professor of Civil En-
gineering in University of West Virginia 1891-1893. In
1945 the Rensselaer Polytechnic Institute conferred
on him the Honorary Degree of Doctor of Engineer-
ing. He was secretary of the Local Board of Clay
County, West Virginia, during World War One, was
his party's nominee for Congress 1904. Practiced
law in Clay County 1894-1911. Entered oil business
in 1911. Has been an officer or director of a number
of corporations, among others, the Clay County
Bank; Plymouth Oil Company; Adena Corporation;
Davis Oil Company; Craig Oil Company; and Gos-
horn Oil Company, the last three operating in West
Virginia; the Santa Barbara Oil Company, oper-

ating in California; and the Quincy Oil Company
and Gale Oil Company, operating in Mississippi and
and Texas. He is a director of the Union Mission
and Davis Child Shelter, of Charleston, W. Va.; is
a member of the Elk's Club, is a 32nd degree Mason,
and a Noble of the Mystic Shrine. Between 1886 and
1892 he saw service as a Civil Engineer with the N.
& W. and C. A. & C. Rail Roads, and in the construc-
tion of levees along the Mississippi River. He is
now retired and lives at 1546 Kanawha Boulevard
Charleston, W. Va. He m. (1) Emily MacLane
White, dau. of the eminent geologist, Dr. I. C. White;
and (2) Alma Florence Stephenson, dau. of Thomas
Benton Stephenson and Glendora, his wife; to the
second marriage the following children were born:

(1)   Benton Stephenson, b. Nov. 28, 1902; d. May 1,
1938; m. Mar. 17, 1933 Imogene Coleman, dau. Dr.
J. E. Coleman, of Fayetteville, W. Va.
Issue:
(a)   Henry Bedinger Davenport, III, b. Feb. 28,
1936.

(2)   Braxton, b. Sept. 29, 1909, m. Dec. 19, 1934, Marjorie Chambers, of Princeton, W. Va., dau. Mr. and
Mrs. J. S. Chambers. He was educated at the University of Virginia and University of West Virginia,
where he received B.S. and M.A. degrees, respectively; and spent one year in France studying its
language and literature. He enlisted in U. S. Navy in
World War Two, and rose to the rank of Lieutenant

Commander. At close of the war he was placced on inactive duty.

(d)   IV. Amelia Field Davenport (196) b. Feb. 24, 1868; m. May, 1890, Col. Catesby Woodford, of Bourbon Co., Ky., Master of Raceland Stock Farm where many fine race horses have been bred. He died April, 1923, since which time Mrs. Woodford has continued to live at Raceland.

(e)   V. Braxton Davenport (197) b. Dec. 2, 1873; d. Oct. 13, 1900; unmarried. Was educated at University of West Virginia, from which he graduated in 1893 with degree of Bachelor of Science. He studied law at University of Virginia, under Dr. John B. Minor, and in 1895 settled at Cleveland, Ohio, in the practice of his profession, under Judge J. H. Collins, Chief Counsel of the B. & O. Rail Road. He died Oct. 13, 1900 of pneumonia. While at college he won distinction as an author and orator. He received at the University of West Virginia the Richard Randalph MacMahon prize on his essay on the "Religion of Shakespeare". Among his writings was a very complete essay on the John Brown raid. He was the author of numerous articles, essays and poems. He died at the early age of twenty-seven years, mourned by a devoted family and a large circle of friends and admirers. He is buried by the side of his father and mother in the Davenport lot in Edgehill Cemetery at Charles Town, W. Va. His tombstone, erected by his father, bears the inscription:

"With thee, my son, perished many hopes".

II. Frances Williams (198) only daughter of Col. Braxton Davenport (46) ad Elizabeth Bedinger, his wife, b. Dec. 6, 1834; d. Oct. 21, 1909; m. Col. John Thomas Gibson, May 9, 1855; b. Jan. 3, 1825; d. Jan. 29, 1904. Issue:

(a)   I. Braxton Davenport Gibson (199) b. Aug. 13, 1856; d. Aug. 14, 1946, at the age of 90 years, 1 day. He was a Mason of high degree, viz: Grand Master of the Grand Lodge of West Virginia; Grand Commander of the Grand Commandery of Knights Templar; Thirty-third Degree Mason. He was educated at the University of Virginia as a lawyer, and practiced some years before his retirement. He served several terms in the Legislature of West Virginia. He married Mary Holliday Mason Dec. 15, 1897. She d.   She was the dau. of Dr. Gerald F. Mason, and Margaret Holliday, his wife, who was a sister of former Governor Fred W. M. Holliday, of Virginia.

Issue:

Margaret Holliday, b. 1901; d. June 13, 1903; unmarried.

(b)   II. Elizabeth Bedinger Gibson, b. Nov. 3, 1859; d. June 25, 1895; unmarried.

(c)   III. Susan Gregg Gibson (200), b. Aug. 6, 1866; lives at Charles Town, W. Va.

(d)   IV. Annie Shepherd Gibson (201), b. 1868; d. ____ 194_; m. William Bainbridge Packette (202), Dec.

26, 1894; he was b. 1854, and d. 1934.

Issue:

(a) John T. Gibson Packette, b. Jan. 15, 1898; d. 1900.

(b) Frances Davenport Packette (203), b. July 28, 1901; m. Augustine Jaquelin Todd.
They live in Washington City, but have a country place near Charles Town, W. Va.

THE STRODE LINE.

1. Sir William Strode, had son
2. John, who had son
3. Edward. He m. Eleanor _____.

Issue:

(a) Susanna, b. 1721.

(b) Edward, b. 1723; d. 1749; unmarried.

(e) James Strode (known as Captain James Strode), b. 1727; d. 1795.
m. (1) Ann Forman Bowman, widow (1721-1786)
m. (2) Chloe Chenowith, b. 1734; and
m. (3) Elizabeth Fryat, she d. 1810.
Children of first Wife:

(1) Susanna, b. 1756; m. James Magowan.

(2) Phoebe, b. 1757; m. Capt. Josiah Swearingen.

(3) Eleanor, b. 1760; m. Capt. Abraham Shepherd.

(4) Rachel, b. Oct. 19, 1762; m. Major Henry Bedinger (206).
Their dau. Elizabeth m. Col. Braxton Davenport (46)
Children of last couple:

(a) Henry B. Davenport, Sr. b. Sept. 9, 1831; d. Sept. 15, 1901; m. Martha I. Clay, b. Feb. 1, 1832; d. May 28, 1908.

(b) Frances Williams, who m. Col. John T. Gibson.

NOTE:

After Capt. Strode's death in 1795 his widow m. Magnus Tate, Jr.

Capt. James Strode was a man of distinction in Berkeley County.

1. He was commissioned Captain of the Militia of Berkeley County, Jan. 17, 1775 by John, Earl of Dunmore; Baron Fincastle, etc.

2. He was commissioned Captain of the Militia of Frederick County, Virginia, April 3, 1771, by William Nelson, President of His Majesty's Council.

(Above commission in my possession.)

Sir William Strode, above, was a member of the Star Chamber in England, and participated in the trial of Charles 1st, whose death warrant he signed. The Strodes were Huguenots, and Sir John Strode, Earl of Strigal, came over with William the Conquerer in 1066.

THE BEDINGER LINE.

Adam Burdinger (204) (afterward changed to Bedinger) migrated from Dorschel, in the Principality of Lichenstein, near Strasburg, in the Province of Alsace, in 1734, and landed at Philadelphia. He shortly moved to Lancaster County, Pennsylvania, and took up land on the Conowaga River. At the time of the migration his son, Nicholas, was eleven years old, and son Heinrich (205) was eight years old. George Michael was six years old, and Peter was four years old.

In 1752 Heinrich (205) married Magdalena von Schlegle (afterward changed to Slagel).

Issue of Heinrich Bedinger (205) and Magdalena von Slagle, his wife:

    I. Henry Bedinger (206) b. Oct. 16, 1753; d. May 14, 1843, at Altona.

    II. Elizabeth (207) b. 1755.

    III. George Michael Bedinger (208) b. Dec. 10, 1756; celebrated Indian fighter.

    IV. John Daniel Bedinger (209) b. Jan. 11, 1761; d. Mar. 17, 1815.

    V. Ann Maria Bedinger (210) b. Feb. 7, 1763; d. Aug. 25, 1804.

    VI. George Jacob Bedinger (211) b. Feb. 5, 1766. Sheriff of Jefferson County.

    VII. Sarah Bedinger (212) b. Sept. 19, 1768; d. Feb. 7, 1792.

    VIII. Solomon Bedinger (213) b. Sept. 19, 1770; d. Sept. 16, 1806.

NOTE:

Sarah Eleanor Bedinger (214) dau. of Oaniel Bedinger (209) was b. 1798; d. Nov. 16, 1816.

Heinrich Bedinger (205) and his family removed to Shepherdstown, Va., now W. Va., in 1762. He and his wife are both buried there in the Old Episcopal Cemetery. He d. Jan. 23, 1772, aged 46 years.

Henry Bedinger (206) was a soldier of the Revolution.

Commissions in the Military Service were issued to him as follows:

No. 1. Third Lieutenant of Rifle Company in Army of the United Colonies, for the Defence of American Liberty, at Philadelphia, July 9, 1776, signed by John Hancock.

No. 2. He was commissioned Captain May 21, 1781, and was assigned to the 5th Va. Regiment. This commission was stolen from my office on or after Oct. 22, 1922.

No. 3. He was commissioned Major of the First Battalion of the 55th Regiment of Virginia Militia May 6, 1793. The commission was signed by Henry Lee, Governor of Virginia.

He was captured by the British at Fort Washington, New York Nov. 16, 1776, and held a prisoner of war until exchanged Nov. 1, 1780, when he returned to Shepherdstown and raised a company of infantry and was appointed its Captain.

He purchased the Protumna Estate, near Martinsburg, in Berkeley County, Va. (now W. Va.) and lived there many years. He served a term as Clerk of County Court of said County. Was original member of the order of Cincinnati, and served as a member of the Legislature of Virginia.

Henry Bedinger (206) b. Oct. 16, 1753; d. May 14, 1843; m. Rachel Strode, dau. of Capt. James Strode and Ann Forman, his wife.

Issue:

I. Nancy m. Col. James S. Swearingen.

II. Sallie died unmarried.

III. Elizabeth m. Col. Braxton Davenport.

IV. Maria m. Col. Samuel Miller; their daughter, Maria, m. Frank Peters, of Philadelphia, Pa.

NOTE:

Magdalena von Slagle, wife of Heinrich Bedinger (205) above, was the dau. of Col. Christopher von Schlegel, who migrated to America from Saxony. He was the son of a German noble, Frederick von Schlegel.

IV. John Daniel Bedinger (known as Daniel Bedinger) third son of Heinrich Bedinger (206) and Magadalena von Schlegel, his wife, was b. Jan. 11, 1761; d. Mar. 17, 1816; m. Sarah Rutherford. He was a soldier of the Revolution. He was captured by the British, along with his brother, Major Henry Bedinger, Nov. 16, 1776, and was confined as a prisoner of war several years. He was a poet of marked ability. Under President John Adams' administration he was Collector of Revenue for the Port of Norfolk. In his letters to his brother, Henry, he often referred to President Adams as "King John". He and his wife had several children.

Issue of Daniel Bedinger and Sarah Rutherford, his wife:

I. Henrietta, m. Edward Jennings Lee; children:

(a) Ida Lee, m. Col. Armstead Thompson Mason Rust, as his second wife—Issue (surname Rust):

I. Armstead.
II. Henrietta Lee, m. Dr. Goldborough.
III. Lilly Southgate.
V. George.
VI. Edward Gray.
VII. Henry Bedinger, lives in Pittsburgh, Pa.

VIII. William Fitzhugh.
IX. Edward Jennings.
X. Ellsworth Marshall.
XI. Daughter, died in infancy.
XII. Sterling Murray, lives in Pittsburgh, Pa.

Children of Col. A. T. M. Rust and his first wife, Lilly Southgate Laurena, of Long Island, N. Y.
(1) Armstead d. 2 years old.
(2) Lawrence.
(3) Frederick.
(4) Rebecca.

"Henry Bedinger Rust, brother of Henrietta Bedinger Lee, my grand-mother, m. Margaret Rust, my father's sister. Their dau. Virginia, m. ____ Michie, of Charlottesville, Va. Their three sons, Thomas, George and Armstead, live in Charlottesville—Thomas, Jr., son of Thomas, is a lawyer and lives in Pittsburgh".

Foregoing from letter of Sterling Murray Rust to J. E. Bedinger, dated Oct. 24, 1934.

II. Virginia m. William Lucas, of Rion Hall, Jefferson Co. W. Va. They had issue, among others:

(1) Daniel Bedinger Lucas, the "Poet Laureate of the Shenandoah Valley". He was a Judge of the Supreme Court of Appeals of West Virginia. He was an erudite scholar, a historian and a lawyer of fine ability. He was a master of correct English, and his essays and writings were models of chaste and elegant composition. He was b. Mar. 16, 1936 at Rion Hall, and d. there July 24, 1909. He m. Miss Lena Brooke, b. 1838; d. 1923, sister of St. George Tucker Brooks, the eminent law professor. They had one child, a daughter, Virginia, b. 1872, a scholary woman, a poetess and writer of marked ability, who met an untimely death at the entrance of Rion Hall, when the automobile she was driving was hit by a large truck. This sad event occurred on the _____ day of _____, 1929.

(2) Virginia Lucas, sister of Judge Daniel B. Lucas, was a woman of ability. She left behind some beautiful poems. She d. in the early bloom of life.

III. Henry Bedinger, son of Daniel Bedinger and Sarah Rutherford, his wife, was a member of Congress, and was U. S. Minister to Denmark. While in that country a daughter was born, who was named "Danske", after the country to which he was accredited. She married Stephen Dandridge. She was a poetess and historian. Among her works were "Biography of George Michael Bedinger",

"Historic Shepherdstown"; "Joy, and other Poems". She was b. ____; d. ____;

IV. Elizabeth Bedinger, daughter of Daniel Bedinger, m. Thornton Washington.

THE SHEPHERD LINE.

Abraham Shepherd, b. Nov. 10, 1754; d. Sept. 7, 1822; m. Dec. 27, 1780 Eleanor Strode, dau. Capt. James Strode and Ann Forman, his wife. She was b. June 27, 1760; d. Sept. 23, 1853. Abraham Shepherd was a son of Thomas and Eliza (Van Metre) Shepherd.

Issue of Abraham Shepherd and Eleanor Strode, his wife:

I. James Strode, b. 1782; d. 1789.

II. Rezin Davis, b. Aug. 1, 1784; d. Nov. 10, 1865, m. Lucy Gorham, of Boston, Mass. b. 1789; d. 1814.

Children of last couple:

(a) James Harvey.

(b) Anne.

(c) Eliza.

(d) Charles Moses.

(e) Ellen b.   m.   Gorham Brooks (3 children.)

III. Abraham, Jr. b. June 1787; d. Oct. 1853; m. Feb. 10, 1813 Ellen Peck, of Staunton, Va. b. 1794.

Issue:

(a) James Harvey, b. 1823; m. Florence Hamtramck.

(b) Catherine   m. Robert A. Lucas.

(c) Frances R. m. Robert McMurran.

(d) Ellen

(e) Henry St. John.

(f) William Meade.

(g) Robert F. d. in Civil War.

(h) Valeria b. ____ m. Carter.

(i) Alex H. d. in Civil War.

(j) Lucy.

(k) Mary.

IV. James Harvey, b. May 5, 1790; d. 1837; unmarried.

 V. Henry S. b. Jan. 1793; d. Oct. 1870; m. May 7, 1822; Fannie E. Briscoe, dau. Dr. John and Eleanor (Magruder) Briscoe, b. May 7, 1800; d. ____. Children:

(a) Mary Eleanor, b. July 1824; d. Aug. 1825.

(b) Rezin Davis, b. July 1826; d. Nov. 1862, m. Elizabeth Stockton Boteler.

Children: Fannie, Alexander and Davis.

(c) Ann Elizabeth, b. Aug. 1828; d. 1838.

(d) Henry, Jr. b. June 13, 1831; d. Sept. 30, 1891, m. Azemia McLean, dau. W. J. McLean, of New Irleans, La.

Issue:

(1) Rezin D. b. 1860. He lives at Hollywood, Cal. d. July 1948; m. (1) Marie Prescott and (2) Odette Tyler. "R. D." Shepherd was a famous actor. He took the name "McLean" (his mother's name) as his stage name. Both of his wives were famous actresses. His last important role was in the Mission Play, at Los Angeles, Cal. where he headed the cast.

(2) Henry Shepherd, III. b. 1868; d. Mar. 1896;

killed in R.R. accident at Shenandoah Junction, W. Va. He m. Miss ____ Rinehart. After his death his widow m. R. C. Ringgold, of Shepherdstown.

(3) William J. Shepherd, b. 1870; d.

(4) Augustus M. Shepherd, b. 1875; d.

(e) John Shepherd, b. June 9, 1833; d. June 20, 1879; unmarried.

(f) Abraham, b. Mar. 21, 1836; m. Eliz. Williams Shepherd.

(g) James Truro, b. Aug. 21, 1839.

VI. Anne, b. June 13, 1796; d. 1866; m. Jan. 17, 1827, Dr. Wm. Thomas Hammond—one child—Mary.

VII. Eliza, b. July 26, 1799; d. Aug. 25, 1833; m. Edmund Jennings Lee, as his first wife. He was b. May 31, 1797; d. 1877 at "Leeland", Jefferson Co. W. Va. Children:

(a) Ellen, b. 1824; d. 1865.

(b) Charles, b. 1826.

VIII. Charles Moses, b. April 11, 1800; d. Oct. 1851; m. Margaret Hook, dau. Capt. John Hook.

Issue:

(a) Harriet.

(b) Richard.

(c) Charles.

NOTE:

Henry Shepherd, Jr., son of Henry S. and Fannie (Briscoe) Shepherd, who was born June 13, 1831, was a man of large wealth. He owned the celebrated Estate known as "Wild Goose", near Shepherdstown, W. Va., and lived there in regal style until his death September 30, 1891. He died in his carriage driving from Shepherdstown to Wild Goose. He made his fortune in the cotton brokerage business in New Orleans, La.

THE MANNING LINE.

(1) Edward Fitz-Randolph, Immigrant ancestor; m. May 10, 1637 at Scituate, Mass., Elizabeth Blossom, dau. of Thomas and Annie Blossom; moved to Piscataway, N. J. 1669; d. 1675.

(2) Joseph Fitz-Randolph, son of (1) above; b. 1657; m. Hanna Congers.

(3) Joseph Fitz-Randolph, Jr., son of (2) above; b. 1691; m. Rebecca Drake.

(4) Grace Fitz-Randolph, dau. of (3) above; m. James Manning; b. 1700, grand-son of Jeffrey Manning.

(5) Jeremiah Manning, son of (4) above; b. 1736; m. 1758 Ursula Drake.

(6) Ursula Manning, dau. of (5) above; m. Phineas Manning, a relative whose grand-mother was Prudence Fitz-Randolph, dau. of Joseph Fitz-Randolph (2) above.

(7) Thomas Jefferson Manning, b. 1803; d. 1857, was son of Phineas (6) and Ursula Manning above. He m. 1840 Frances R. Jack, of Jefferson Co. Va., dau. of Julia A. Davenport, who m. Capt. Robert F. Jack. She was a dau. of Major Abraham Davenport (5) and wife, Frances Williams (40).

The foregoing information given me by Robert Jack
Manning.

IV. Julia A. Davenport (49) dau. of Major Abraham
Davenport (5) and Frances Williams (40), his wife,
was b. Oct. 3, 1797; d. Feb. 11, 1854; m. Robert F.
Jack. Their dau. Frances Rebecca Jack, b. Dec. 3,
1818; d. Feb. 25, 1855; m. Capt. Thomas J. Manning,
of the U. S. Navy. He d. Jan. 6, 1857, aged 54 years,
Issue:

I. Charles J. Manning (215); b. June 21, 1842; d.
Feb. 4, 1903; m. (1) Mary E. Cowan, dau. of J. N.
Cowan, of Rockingham County, Va., May 4, 1864;
and (2) Minnie F. Williams, b. 1858; d. 1922; m.
Nov. 12, 1890 at Bridgewater, Va. Wife (1) died
May 17, 1889.

Issue of First Marriage:

(a) Charles Cowan (216), b. Aug. 28, 1865; d. Jan.
1943; m. Lura Patterson, b.   d.
Issue:

(1) Robert Jack Manning (217), b. Aug. 29, 1910; m.
____ ; employee of du Pont Company, at Wilmington,
Del. Chemist graduate V.M.I. Served in Aerial
Division second World War, Rank of Major. Mar-
ried, has one son. And (2), Charles C. Manning,
Jr., (218) b. Oct. 12, 1916; unmarried. Educated
in law, University of Va. Lives at Wilmington,
Del.

II. George U. Manning, b. Dec. 15, 1844; a soldier in the
Confederacy. Killed in action. Unmarried.

III. Frank Jack Manning (219) b. Oct. 29, 1848; d. 1906; m. Laura A. Cowan; b. Jan. 30, 1849; d. Jan. 30, 1929.
Issue:

(1) Alice (220), b. Mar. 1, 1869; d. Dec. 24, 1903; m. Lee Pryor.
Issue: Alice Earl Pryor, b.   m.   and lives in Boston, Mass. m. Roscoe Hayes; 1 child.

(2) Delia (221) b. 1871; d. July 9, 1947; m. Rolfe Gerhardt, who d. Jan. 1826. Issue none.

(3) Frank, Jr. (222) b.   d. 1899; unmarried. Was a soldier in the Spanish war.

(4) Antoinette (223) b.   m. Clarence L. Walsh; lives in Charleston, W. Va. He d. April 29, 1948. Issue none.

(5) Thomas J. Jr. (224) b.   d. Jan. 26, 1929; m. (1) ____ (2) Mary McCoughtry.
Issue none.

(6) Amelia (225) b.   d. Dec. 1, 1947. m. S. Preston Smith.
Issue:

(1) S. Preston (Reddy) Jr. (226) b.   m.   2 children.
(2) Manning (227) b.   m.   2 children.

NOTE:

S. Preston Smith, Jr. (226) rose to rank of Major in the U. S. Army World War II.

CHENOWITH LINE.

Arthur Chenowith, m. Mary Calvert, dau. of Cecil Calvert. Lord Baltimore, will recorded in Baltimore 1802.

Issue:

(a) John, Sr. m. (1) Hannah Cromwell; (2) ___ (name not given).

(b) Samuel m. (1) Patience Cromwell and (2) Elizabeth Mary Cromwell and (3) (Name not given).

Issue: John Chenowith, Sr. and Hannah, his wife,

1. Richard. Founder of Louisville, Ky.
2. Thomas.
3. Arthur (for issue see below)
4. Hannah.
5. John Chenowith, Jr., son of John, Sr., above and Hannah, his wife, m. Mary Davenport, of Charlestown, Va. (now W. Va.) b. 1775; d. 1865, dau. Dr. John Davenport. They lived at "Stony Mead", near Bunker Hill, Berkeley County, Va., nine miles from Winchester. John Chenowith was b. 1770; d. 1865 at Green Castle, Ind. Will recorded there.

Issue:

1. Ellen.
2. John W.
3. Alfred G.
4. George Davenport.
5. Rebecca.
6. Mary Davenport.
7. Richard W.
8. Benjamin.

9. Margaret.

The family of Arthur Chenowith, son of John, Sr.

1. John.
2. Richard.
3. Sarah Taylor.
4. Ruth Oufett (Offutt).
5. Arthur.
6. Joshua.
7. Chloe Chenowith, m. Capt. James Strode as 2nd wife.
8. Hannah Harris.

Will of John, Sr. is recorded at Winchester, Va.

John's wife was dau. of Wm. Cromwell. The first Wm. Cromwell came over in the Bonnie Eaton, March 11, 1671. His brother, John Richard and a sister came together. Sailor's list at Annapolis, Md. Wm. Cromwell was a brother of Oliver Cromwell. The first John Chenowith I have notes of came from Isle of Wight in 1652. He was a Welsh nobleman. He sailed on the Ark and Dove. These two small vessels brought them over with _____ Calvert and the Cromwells. John had a sister who m. a Cromwell, supposed to be a daughter or sister of Oliver. John, Sr. had two sons, Arthur and Richard. This Arthur, the father of John, who m. Hannah Cromwell, is the son of the first John. Above imperfect notes given me by C. F. Robey. John Chenowith, Sr., will dated 1814, was recorded in Berkeley County, Sept. 11, 1820. In it he mentions John Strode and Nancy Edmunds "children of 'My Chloe'," and her husband, Capt. James Strode

Children mentioned in above will:

Joshua, John, Richard, Sarah Taylor, Hanna Harris, Ruth Offit and Arthur. He also mentions his grand-daughter, Sarah Thomas. Will Records Berkeley Co. Va. Book 6, p. 316.

NOTE:

Mary Davenport, dau. John Davenport, b. 1775; d. 1865 at Green Castle, Ind. m. John Chenowith, son of John and Hannah (Cromwell) Chenowith, of Berkeley Co., Va. He was b. 1770; d. 1865. Removed to Indiana in 1861.

Following notes given me by Mrs. W. T. Killam of Laredo, Texas.

KILLAM & CHENOWETH FAMILIES.

Nancy Overall b. 9-1-1810; d. 7-24-1879 m. Jan. 30, 1830, Lloyd Belt Magruder, b. 1-1-1800; d. 4-26-1877. Their dau. Julia Catherine Magruder b. 10-9-1845, d. 10-14-1900, m. David Thomas Killam Oct. 22, 1867, who was b. 5-16-1843 d. 7-27-1927. He was son of Winfield Scott Killam, b. _____ d. 1849, and Mary McClay, his wife, b. _____ d. 1874.

Their son William Thomas Killam b. 8-10-1870. He m. 11-27-1895, Julia Wright Chenoweth b. Dec. 8, 1871.

Issue:

(a) David Chenoweth Killam b. 9-9-1896 d. 9-26-1918. He was private U. S. Marine Corp. 1918.

(b) Tully Bernard Killam b. 3-1-1898.

(c) William Thomas Killam b. 9-14-1900, d. 11-28-1902.

(d) Julia Catherine Killam, b. 1-23-1904, m. Roy Henry 12-30-1928.

Ancestors of Julia Wright Chenoweth Killam.

Ella Crume b. 5-25-1851, d. 10-20-1929 m. 9-21-1869. Alfred Hamlin Chenoweth, b. 12-17-1846, d. 11-28-1887.

Ella Crume was dau. Jonathan Wright Crume b. 10-26-1821, d. 1-28-1892, m. 4-14-1842 Leah Jane Dryden b. 2-23-1824, d. 2-21-1898. These two were parents of **Ella Crume.**

ANCESTORS OF ALFRED HAMLIN CHENOWETH.

Abraham Davenport, Sr. b. 1714, d. 1789 m. Mary Simms about 1845. Their son, John Davenport, b. 1753, d. 1815, m. Eleanor Harris, b. 1768. Their dau. Mary Davenport, b. 1781, d. 1865, m. 11-22-1798, John Chenoweth, Jr. b. 3-8-1775, d. 8-18-1865. Their son Alfred Griffith Chenoweth, b. 2-9-1809, d. 4-25-1864, m. 2-15-1838. Catherine Ann Peel, b. 6-1-1812, d. 1-14-1881.

These last two were the parents of Alfred Hamlin Chenoweth, the father of Julia Wright Chenoweth above (Mrs. W. T. Killam).

THE ROBERT SCOTT FRANKLIN LINE.

Mary Ann Scott, b. 1804; d.   m. Sept. 25, 1827. William Bussard, b. Oct. 29, 1804; d. Jan. 4, 1879. He was a son of David Bussard, and grand-son of David and Sophia Bussard. They were Huguenots. William Bussard was

m. twice. He m. (2) Eliza Lee Bell, dau. of Charles Bell, of Fauquier County, Va. He had his name changed by Act of the Legislature from Bussard to Franklin. He graduated with A. B. degree from University of New Jersey in 1822. He got his M. A. degree in 1825. Studied law with Francis Scott Key. Moved to Chillicothe, Ohio in 1831; practiced law, taught school, etc., elected Auditor of Ross County, Ohio in 1840, and served until 1858. Made Registrar of the Land Office 1858, and served until 1876, when the office was abolished. He d. 1879.

Issue:

Charles Love Franklin, b. Aug. 10, 1839; d. Sept. 18, 1874; m. July 18, 1864 Sarah B. Thatcher, dau. Dr. N. W. Thatcher and his wife, Sarah Bedinger Swearingen, dau. Col. James Strode Swearingen. He graduated from U. S. Naval Academy 1854, and was appointed Midshipman; made Lieutenant 1861; Lieutenant Commander 1865, and Commander 1872. Died of Yellow Fever at Pensacola, Florida, Sept. 18, 1874.

Issue of Commander Charles L. Franklin and Sarah Bedinger Swearingen, his wife:

1. Marion, b. May 13, 1866, d. Dec. 16, 1944 in Florida.
2. Charles Love, b. Sept. 30, 1868; died infant 1869.
3. William Wallace, b. Jan. 15, 1870. Lives at Bogota, U.S.C.
4. Robert Scott, b. Feb. 1, 1872; single; d. at Charleston, W. Va. Apr. 7, 1945.

NOTE:

William Wallace Franklin, above, has two sons at Chi-

cago, in U. S., viz: Charles G. Franklin and _____
Franklin.

Above information given me by Ruffner Payne April 10, 1945.

SWEARINGEN FAMILY LINE.

NOTE:

Following notes given me by Mr. Henry Bedinger Swearingen, of Circleville, Ohio, September 23, 1947.

Josiah Swearingen, oldest son of Van and Sarah Swearingen.

   I. Line of descent: Gerritt Van Swearingen b. in Holland abt. 1635. Came to America 1657; m. Barbara de Barrette 1659; she d. 1671; de d. at St. Marys, Md. 1698.

  II Thomas Swearingen, Sr., son of Gerritt, b. 1665; m. Jane _____; d. 1710.
Thomas Swearingen, Jr., son of Thomas, Sr. b. 1688; m. Lydia Riley; she d. 1730.

  III. Van Swearingen, second son of Thomas and Lydia Riley Swearingen; b. May 22, 1719. Removed to Shepherdstown, Va. (now W. Va.) 1834; m. June 19, 1743 Sarah Swearingen, dau. of his Uncle Van Swearingen (Maryland "Van").

  IV. Josiah Swearingen, b. May 23, 1744; m. Jan. 5, 1777 Phoebe Strode, dau. Capt. James Strode and Anne Forman, his wife. Josiah d. Aug. 1795; wife b. Dec. 8, 1757; d. July 8, 1786. He was private in

Capt. Hugh Stevenson's Company of Riflemen, with whom he marched to seige of Boston in 1775. He was later a Captain of Militia to end of the war (revolution). County Surveyor of Berkeley Co., Va., etc.

Issue: Surname Swearingen.

 I. Eleanor, b. Sept. 27, 1777; m. Dec. 13, 1796; d. Dec. 24, 1848.

 II. Thomas Van, b. Dec. 19, 1779; m. Apr. 6, 1806; d. Sept. 29, 1863.

 III. James Strode, b. Feb. 3, 1782; m. Nov. 4, 1811; d. Feb. 3, 1864.

 IV. Samuel, b. 1784; m. (1) Phoebe Crouse, (2) Nancy Calhoun, d. 1832.

Eleanor, above, m. Thomas Worthington Dec. 13, 1796. He was b. ____; d. ____; was United States Senator, and later Governor of Ohio.

Issue: Surname Worthington.

 I. Mary Tiffin, b. 1797; m. Mar. 1816; d. 1836.

 II. Sarah, b. 1800; m. (1) Edward King, (2) ___ Peter.

 III. James Taylor, b. 1802; m. 1828; d.____

 IV. Thomas, Col. U. S. Army; d. 1884.

 V. Eleanor Strode, b. ___; m. ___ Dr. Arthur Watts.

 VI. Margaret, b. July 25, 1811; m. Apr. 24, 1839; d. Mar. 1863.

 VII. William, d. ____.

 VIII. Elizabeth Rachel, b. 1815; m. Chas. R. Pomeroy.

 IX. Francis, b. ____; d. ____.

Mary Tiffin, above, m. David B. Macomb; she d.

1836; he d. 1837, at Lynchburg, Texas.

Issue: Surname Macomb.

I. Eleanor Worthington, m. ____; d. 1839.

II. Sarah, d. in infancy.

III. Thomas Worthington, b. 1820; d. 1874.

IV. Louise, d. 1889, unmarried.

V. Morris M. died an infant.

VI. Mary Worthington, m. 1846; d. 1851.

VII. David B. b. Feb. 27, 1827; m. July 8, 1859; d. ____.

Sarah Worthington, dau. Eleanor Swearingen and Thomas Worthington, her husband, b. 1800; m. (1) Edward King. He d. and she m. (2) _____ Peter, Consul General at Philadelphia for the British Government. She was the author of "The Worthington Memoir", and the book "In Winter We Flourish", is a biography of her.

Issue by King:

I. Rufus, b. ____; d. ____; he was an eminent lawyer in Ohio.

II. James Taylor, b. 1802; m. (1) 1828 Julia Galloway, who d. 1856. He m. (2) Mrs. Reed, who survived him.

Issue by Julia Galloway:

I. Elizabeth, died an infant.

II. Mary, died unmarried.

III. Martha, died an infant.

IV. Thomas, died 1891, unmarried.

V. James, d. in Army 1863.

VI. Eleanor, d. unmarried.

VII. Julia, m. Henry McDonald.
    Issue:
  I. Eleanor Worthington.
  II. Henry.
  III. Richard T. b. ____; m. Arabella Piatt, dau. of General A. Saunders Piatt.
    Issue:
    I. James.
    II. Anna.
    III. Elizabeth.
    IV. Abram Saunders.
    V. Eleanor Martha.
    VI. Julian.
    VII. Eloise.
VIII. Jacob.

Thomas Worthington, son of Eleanor Swearingen and Thomas Worthington was Colonel in U. S. Army in Civil War. He d. 1884.

Eleanor Strode, dau. Eleanor and Thomas Worthington, b. ____; m. Dr. Arthur Watts.
    Issue: Surname Watts.
  I. Eleanor, b. ____; m. General A. Saunders Platt.
  II. Margaret.
  III. Thomas, d. 1883.

Margaret, dau. Eleanor and Thomas Worthington, b. at Adena July 25, 1811; m. Apr. 24, 1836 Edward Deering Mansfield. She d. Mar. 1863. He was b. 1800; d. 1880; was Editor Cincinnati Gazette, and was a noted writer.
    dington.

Issue: Surname Mansfield.

I. Elizabeth Phipps, b. Dec. 14, 1843; m. Dec. 7, 1864. Rev. A. S. Dudley.

II. Eleanor Strode, b. Nov. 1845; m. twice.

III. Francis Worthington, b. Nov. 11, 1848, graduate West Point.

IV. Margaret Edith, b. Feb. 20, 1853.

Issue of Elizabeth Phipps and Rev. A. S. Dudley.

I. Elizabeth Mansfield, m. Mar. 1889 Geo. E. Coddingto.

II. Edith.

III. Helen.

IV. Margaret.

V. Adolphous.

Eleanor Strode Mansfield, above, m. (1) Sept. 1873 Charles Moulton, who d. 1874. She then m. August 1880 Rev. Edward T. Swiggett.

Issue of second marriage:

I. Edward Mansfield Swiggett.

II. Douglas Worthington Swiggett.

Elizabeth Rachel, dau. Eleanor and Thomas Worthington, b. Berkeley Co. Va. 1815; m. Chas. R. Pomeroy. He founded City of Pomeroy, Ohio.

Issue: Surname Pomeroy.

I. Eleanor, m. Dan. E. Smith. She d. 1862 (See below).

II. John, m. Julia Potter. Issue: Elizabeth and Anne P.

III. Sarah Wm. Fred O. Willman (See below).

IV. Charles, soldier of U. S. killed at siege of Atlanta.

V. Richard, m. Mary Lewis. Lived at New Orleans, La.

VI. Caroline, m. Ben Onderdonk. Issue: Maurice and Eleanor.

VII. Arthur, soldier of U. S. in Civil War. Died in Arkansas.

Issue of Eleanor and Daniel E. Smith.

Son, E. S. Smith, name changed to Worthington by legislature. m. Anne Atwater. Lived in Sandusky, Ohio.

Elizabeth Worthington, b. ____; m. ____ and as Countess Elizabeth W. de la Marque, lived at Boulonge, Sur Seine, France 1893.

Issue of Sarah W. Pomeroy and her husband, Fred O. Willman:

I. Charles Willman.

II. Eleanor Willman.

III. Edith Willman.

Thomas Van Swearingen, son of Josiah, b. Dec. 19, 1779; m. Apr. 6, 1806; d. Sept. 29, 1863 in Illinois. He m. Theodocia Goodale; she d. Apr. 6, 1832.

Issue:

I. Samuel G. b. 1807; m. (1) Sarah Caldwell (2) Amanda Cunningham.

II. Cynthia, b. Oct. 1808; m. Matthew Gooding. No issue.

III. Joseph, b. 1812; m. Elizabeth Wright Lockwood; d. 1856.

IV. Elizabeth Phelps, b. Oct. 1814; m. Jan. 1836 Rev. Nelson Hawley.

V. Martha Jane, b. July 12, 1823; m. Chester H. Fitch. She d. 1863.

VI. Maria Theodocia.

Issue of Samuel G. and Sarah Caldwell Swearingen:

I. Lincoln G. b. Dec. 7, 1833; m. May 1, 1860 Mary Palmater.

II. Sarah C.

III. Cynthia G.

IV. Theodore P.

Issue of Lincoln G. and Mary Palmater Swearingen:

I. Oscar L. b. Feb. 2, 1861; m. (1) Abbie McKibben, and (2) Rachel Miller.

Issue by first marriage:

I. M. Allena.

II. S. Beulah.

III. Herschel M.

Issue by Second marriage:

I. Mabel L.

II. Sarah C. m. E. E. Murphy.

III. Cynthia G. d. 1856.

IV. Theodore P. b. 1848; m. Kate Meisenhelter.

Issue of last couple:

I. Minnie.

II. Frank.

Issue of Joseph Swearingen and Elizabeth W. Lockwood, his wife:

I. Two boys died in uniform.
II. Virginia, b. ____; m. Fred P. Moffett.
Issue: Mildred, Bruce F., Cady J., Burnham A.
III. Clara G. b. ____; m. Geo. Bostwich Goodrich. Issue:
I. Omar.
II. Maynard.
III. Clara, lived at Mankato, Kansas.
Issue of Elizabeth Phelps and husband, Rev. Nelson Hawley:
I. Thomas Swearingen Hawley, b. 1837; d. 1890.
II. Amos Augustus Hawley.
III. Maria Denning Hawley, m. Wm. Reed.
IV. Helen Frances Hawley.
V. Theodocia Goodale Hawley.
VI. Eva Belle Hawley, m. Frank D. Turner.
Issue: Frank and Maude.
Dr. Thomas S. Hawley, above, m. 1865 Carrie Joy; d. 1890.
Issue: I. Martha May, b. 1866; m. Geo. D. Meekel.
Issue: Son, George D., Lizzie, Dr. Nelson, Thomas, Wilden H., and Carrie Belle.
Issue of Maria D. Hawley and husband, William Reed:
I. Ritta, b. 1868; d. 1887.
II. Eugene Orr.
III. Frank Goodale, b. 1874; d. 1893.

IV. William Phelps.

V. Helen F. Hawley, m. Harvey Johnson. No issue.

Issue of Martha Jane and Chester H. Fitch:

I. Alice Gooding, died in infancy.

II. Ida H. Died in infancy.

III. Thomas Van S. Died in infancy.

IV. Emma Florence, m. Joel M. Longnecker.

V. Theodore Goodale, m. India E. Turner.

VI. Susan Rosabella, m. Dec. 1872 B. F. McCord:

Issue: Anna and Chester.

VII. Theodocia Elizabeth, m. Dr. Arthur G. Meserve.

VIII. Martha Jane Hawley, m. Andrew J. Tohill.

Issue of Emma F. and husband, Joel Longnecker:

I. Chester Ralph.

II. Rolla Randolph.

III. Theodore Roy.

IV. Fitch Joel.

V. Florence Gladys.

VI. Theodocia M.

Issue of Theodocia Elizabeth and Dr. Arthur G. Meserve:

I. Ashbel Fitch.

II. Maud.

III. Gladys.

IV. Theodocia.

V. Grace Goodale.

VI. Theodore Decatur.

Issue of Martha Jane Hawley and Andrew J.

Tohill:

I. Chester Fitch.

II. Roy G.

James Strode Swearingen, second son of Josiah, born Berkeley Co. Va. Feb. 3, 1782; m. Nov. 4, 1811 Nancy Bedinger, dau. Major Henry Bedinger and Rachel Strode, his wife. He d. at Chillicothe, Ohio Feb. 3, 1864. Nancy d. Jan. 18, 1858.

Issue: Surname Swearingen.

I. Henry Bedinger, b. at Adena, Nov. 16, 1814; m. Elizabeth Nesbitt Jan. 2, 1850; b. Jan. 3, 1827; d. Feb. 8, 1881; he d. Oct. 15, 1889.

II. Eleanor.

III. Sarah Bedinger.

IV. Virginia.

V. James, b. Oct. 31, 1824; d. Oct. 1834.

VI. Nancy Calhoun, b. Feb. 23, 1823; d. Apr. 17, 1823.

Henry Bedinger Swearingen, above, d. Oct. 15, 1889; his wife b. Jan. 3, 1827; d. Feb. 8, 1881.

Issue of Henry Bedinger and Elizabeth Nesbitt Swearingen:

I. Eleanor Virginia, b. Mar. 26, 1854; m. Oct. 1882 W. Vernon Grant; d. Sept. 1890. One child, Henry W., b. Oct. 8, 1888; m. Lora ____; 2 daughters.

II. James Strode, b. Aug. 19, 1857; m. Nov. 12, 1890 Minerva Anderson.

III. Nancy Nesbitt, b. Dec. 22, 1859; d. May 31, 1887. Educated at Kenyon College, Gambier, Ohio.

IV. Rachel Nesbitt, b. Feb. 1861; d. 1865.

V. John Grant, b. Feb. 24, 1863; d. 1938! d. 1938! m. Nov. 13, 1888 Fannie B. Dent, one child.

VI. Henry Bedinger, b. May 27, 1865; m. Apr. 4, 1894 Louise H. Stewart.

VII. Thomas Townsley, b. Jan. 15, 1868; m. ___; d. ___.

VIII. Mary Scott, b. Mar. 9, 1871; m. Oct. 12, 1893 Wm. A. Hail. Henry W. Grant, son of Eleanor Virginia and W. Vernon Grant, b. Oct. 8, 1888; m. Lora ___; has 2 dau. both married.

Issue of James Strode Swearingen and Minerva Anderson, his wife:

I. Henry Bedinger, b. Aug. 31, 1894; m. Issue: James S. and Nancy.

II. William Fleming, b. Sept. 13, 1895.

III. Sarah, b. Mar. 1897; m. Chas. Pugsley.

John Grant Swearingen, b. Feb. 24, 1863; d. 1938. His wife, Fannie B. Dent, d. ____; left one child, Virginia, b. 1890; m. Edward Strode Thatcher. Issue:

I. Virginia, m. James Brown.

II. Edward S., Jr. m. ____.

III. Ann, m. ____.

IV. John

V. Jeanne, m. Ned Burns.

Henry Bedinger Swearingen and Louise H. Stewart, his wife, she was b. Oct. 12, 1869. Issue:

I. Louise Stewart, b. Aug. 8, 1895; m. Chas. C. Merritt. Issue:

I. William, b. ____.

II. John Henry, b. ____; d. 1926.

III. Geo. Thomas, b. Jan. 15, 1925.

  II. Henry Bedinger, III, b. Sept. 26, 1897. Writes his name "Van" Swearingen.

      Issue of Mary Scott Swearingen and husband, Wm. A. Hail:

    I. Thomas Jules, b. 1894; m. ____; 2 daughters, one married.

  II. Iona, m. ____; a son.

III. Elizabeth, m. ____; a dau. Barbara, and son Garret.

 IV. William A., b. ____;

  V. Virginia, m. Geo. Marshall—4 children.

Eleanor Swearingen, b. May 16, 1816; m. (1) 1842 Dr. John Grant, who d. 1852; and m. (2) Edward Clarkson; she d. June 27, 1879. No issue.

Sarah Bedinger Swearingen, dau. James Strode and Nancy Bedinger Swearingen, b. July 15, 1819; m. Feb. 26, 1840 Nathaniel W. Thatcher, b. May 25, 1807; d. Nov. 11, 1874. She lived all her life at Chillicothe, Ohio, and d. June 7, 1886.

    Issue: Surname Thatcher.

   I. Sarah Bedinger, b. 1841; m. July 18, 1864 Charles L. __ Franklin.

  II. Lucretia M.

III. Virginia S.

 IV. James S.

  V. Nancy Bedinger, d. unmarried.

 VI. Henry A. d. unmarried.

VII. Edward Strobe, b. 1857; m. Margaret Maginnis; 2 children.

Sarah Bedinger, above, b. 1841. Her husband (Franklin) b. ____; d. Sept. 19, 1874. She d. 1930. Their issue:

I. Marian Scott, b. May 16, 1866; d. Dec. 16, 1944.

II. Charles Love, b. Sept. 30, 1868; d. infant.

III. William Woodbridge, b. Jan. 15, 1870. Lives in U. S. of Columbia; m. 2 sons in Chicago, Ill.

IV. Robert Scott, b. Feb. 1, 1872; d. at Charleston, W. Va. April 7, 1945. Never married. Geneologist.

V. Lucretia M. d. unmarried.

VI. Virginia S. b. ____m. Walter Howson.
Issue of last marriage: Surname Howson.

I. John Harold, d. unmarried.

II. James Arthur, and Walter (twins). Last married three times; three children live in Chillicothe. James S. m. Gertrude Adams; son Edward Augustus, lives in Dallas, Texas.

Edward Strode Swearingen, who was born in 1857, m. Margaret Maginnis, and had two children, viz:

I. Col. Edward S. Swearingen, b. ____; m. Virginia, dau. John Grant Swearingen, and has issue. See ante, p. 77.

II. John James Swearingen, b. ____; m. has several children.

Samuel Swearingen, youngest child of Josiah and Phoebe Strode Swearingen, b. 1847; m. (1) Phoebe Crouse; (2) Nancy Calhoun—No Issue. He moved to Ohio 1799. Served as Captain in War of 1812. State Senator from Ross Co. d. 1832.

THE STEPHENSON LINE.

Alexander Stephenson, b.   d.   m. Sarah Ann Ewing. They lived in Nicholas Co., Va.   (Now W. Va.)

Issue (among others):

(1) John Garner Stephenson, b. Oct. 27, 1787; d. May 8, 1857; m. May 14, 1811, Charity Lemasters, b. Nov. 21, 1791; d. May 8, 1870, dau. of Benjamin Lemasters and Rebecca Martin, his wife. Lemasters was a Revolutionary soldier. John Garner Stephenson lived on a farm near Enon, Nicholas Ca., Va. (Now W. Va.) He was an ensign in the war of 1812; later he was Captain of a Virginia Militia Company, and afterwards Colonel of the 126th Regiment, Virginia Militia. He served in the General Assembly of Virginia from December, 1822 to March 1834. For issue, see below:

(2) David Ewing Stephenson, b. Apr. 10, 1801; d. May 13, 1847; m. Nancy Rader, b. 10-23-1809; d. July 29, 1875.

Issue:

(a) Albert, b.   d. 1861; m. Ann McDermott, Nov. 14, 1848; she d.

(b) Electia, d. Jan. 20, 1850, unmarried.

(c) Andrew Jackson Stephenson, b. Apr. 29, 1829; d. Oct. 29, 1903; m. July 24, 1854, Mary Jane Forsythe; b. Mar. 10, 1832; d. May 3, 1923.
For issue, see below:

(d) Sarah Jane, b. June 21, 1831; d. Nov. 2, 1913; m.

Jackson Pettigrew.

(e) George Alexander, b. Jan. 25, 1835; d. Apr. 15, 1886; m. Louise Perkins, Feb. 10, 1858.

(f) Samuel, b. Apr. 13, 1838; d. Aug. 13, 1896; m.
(1) Jeanette McClung Feb. 1865,
(2) Mariah Hutchinson, July, 1872, and
(3) Anne Williams, Sept. 16, 1880.

(g) Elijah B. b. July 1, 1840; d. May 3, 1862; unmarried.

(h) David Benton, b. Mar. 7, 1844; d. June, 1863; unmarried.

Issue of John Garner Stephenson and Charity Lemasters:

(a) Franklin Stephenson, b. Feb. 26, 1812; d. July 12, 1848; m. Oct. 24, 1843 his cousin, Julia Ann Stephenson, b. 1822; d. Nov. 7, 1867.

Issue:

(a) Thomas Benton Stephenson, b. Dec. 26, 1845; d. Feb. 24, 1921; m. Glendora Stephenson, dau. Andrew Jackson Stephenson and Mary Jane, his wife, Oct. 21, 1875. She was b. 4-18-55 and d. 4-2-39.

Issue:

(1) Annie W. b. 9-18-76; d. 9-18-44; m. Patrick M. Summers; b.   d. Jan. 5, 1948.

(2) Alma Florence, b. Aug. 19, 1881; m. Jan. 22, 1902, Henry B. Davenport.

(3) Beatrice, b.   m. J. M. Lorentz.

NOTE: There were two girls born to Thomas Benton

Stephenson, and Glendora, his wife, who died in infancy.

Issue of Annie W. and Patrick M. Summers:

(a) Mary, b. May 22, 1900; m. Ernest K. James, Lawyer. No issue.

(b) John C. b. 6-21-1902; m. Alice Wood.

Issue:

(1) John C., Jr. b. 6-23-37.

(2) Patricia Ann b. 12-16-41.

Issue of Alma F. Stephenson and husband, Henry B. Davenport, b. Feb. 11, 1865; d. (not yet—5-23-48):

(a) Benton Stephenson, b. Nov. 28, 1902; d. May 1, 1938; m. Mar. 17, 1933, Imogene Coleman, dau. Dr. J. S. Coleman, of Fayetteville, W. Va.

Issue: Henry Bedinger Davenport, III. b. Feb. 28, 1936.

(b) Braxton Davenport, b. Sept. 29, 1909; m. Dec. 19, 1934, Marjorie Chambers, dau. J. S. and Alice Wiley Chambers, of Princeton, W. Va.

Issue of Beatrice and J. M. Lorentz:

(a) Henrietta Davenport Lorentz, b. July 1, 1925; m. Joseph Cook, Feb. 7, 1948.

(b) Josephine, b. Jan. 22, 1927; student at W. V. U.

Issue of Andrew Jackson Stephenson, and Mary Jane, his wife, who was dau. of Abraham and Jane Reed Wright Forsythe:

(a) Glendora, b. 4-18-55; d. 4-2-39. See above.

(b) Forsythe, b. Jan. 3, 1857; d. July 8, 1928; unmarried.

(c) Samuel, b. Mar. 10, 1859; d. Nov. 16, 1934; m. Della Vickers Sayre, Widow.

Issue:

(1) Byron, b. Aug. 23, 1897; m.

(2) Ruby, b. Jan. 31, 1899; m. Leslie Egbert 10-26-1922.

Issue:

(a) Constance b. July 1, 1923; m

(b) Leslie F., Jr. b. Sept. 8, 1926

(d) Elijah Loring, b. May 25, 1861; d. 1-17-1942; m. Missouri Young.

Issue:

(a) Garner, b. May 19, 1892; unmarried.

(b) Nona, b. June 17, 1901; m. John Francesa.

(c) Walter E. b. Mar. 9, 1885; d. 1898; accidentally killed.

(d) Mamie B. b. Apr. 4, 1887; d. Sept. 25, 1902.

(e) May, b. Sept. 5, 1889; d. Nov. 23, 1918; m. Robert Shelton; left 2 sons.

(e) Albert Stephenson, b. Oct. 6, 1863; d. May 27, 1934; m. Elizabeth Salisbury. Issue:

(1) Lida, b. Oct. 30, 1887; m. Alex Harrison, had children.

(2) Benjamin, b. Aug. 30, 1889; m. ____ Rhinehart; 6 children.

(3) Hattie, b. July 25, 1891; m. Gus Andrews, 9 children.

(4) Florence, b. Jan. 30, 1893; unmarried.

(5) Andrew Scott, b. Apr. 23, 1895; killed in auto accident Dec. 20, 1935.

(6) Jacob, b. Jan. 25, 1897; dec'd 6-18-37.

(f) Elizabeth Florence, b. Mar. 25, 1866; d. Apr. 17, 1935; m. Apr. 29, 1890, John D. Carden, b. 2-21-64 d. 11-3-29.

Issue:

(1) Stella, b. May 19, 1891; unmarried.

(2) Eston, b. Nov. 1, 1892.

(3) Cecil, b. Dec. 30, 1894.

(4) William, b. Jan. 9, 1897.

(5) Gertrude, b. Mar. 9, 1902.

(6) Charles, b. May 19, _____.

(7) John D., Jr. b. Apr. 29, 1908.

(g) David Homer Stephenson, b. May 22, 1868; m. Lydia Nichols; b.   d. July, 1948.

Issue:

(1) Maud, b. July 1, 1889; d. Feb. 21, 1939; m. Carl Andrews.

Issue:

(a) Eudora, b. Aug. 2, 1923.

(b) Lois, b. Nov. 20, 1926.

(2) Hettie, b. May 1, 1891; m. Maxwell Campbell, May 4, 1912.

(3) Pearl, b. Nov. 26, 1895; d. May 1, 1938, unmarried.

(4) Freda, b. Sept. 14, 1897; m. K. Wilmans. No issue.

(5) Chilton, b. Apr. 13, 1892; d. 1945; m. E. Atkins; 6 children.

(6) Newton, b. Apr. 8, 1900; m. Chessie Robertson May, 1923; 2 sons.

(h) Benjamin L. Stephenson, b.   died an infant.

(i) Eston Byrne, b. May 13, 1873; d. Apr. 17, 1926; m. Lydia Downey. Issue:

Eston Byrne Stephenson, Jr. He is Asst. Atty. Gen. of W. Va.

NOTES:

Andrew Jackson Stephenson, 1829-1903, was a man of distinction. He served a term as Sheriff of Nicholas County, and was Clerk of the County Court of Clay County, for about thirty years. During the same time he served as Clerk of the Circuit Court of said County for about twenty-four years.

Thomas Benton Stehenson, 1846-1921, was for more than forty years a merchant and banker at Clay, W. Va. He was the founder of the Clay County Bank, and was its President over twenty years. In politics he was a militant and ardent democrat. He was a Noble of the Mystic Shrine, and a 32nd degree mason.

Three of Andrew Jackson Stephenson's sons, viz:

Albert, Loring and Homer served as Sheriff of Clay County; and one of them, Homer, also served as Sheriff of Kanawha County. Another son, Dr. Eston Byrne Stephenson, served on the Board of Control, and also on the State Road Commission of West Virginia.

NOTES ON REV. JOHN DAVENPORT,
OF CONNECTICUT.

Figures ( ) refer to numbers in Dr. Benedict Davenport's Book.

Henry Davenport (58) m. (1) Winifred Barnabus and (2) Elizabeth dau. of Thomas of Glaustershire.

Issue of first marriage:

(a) Christopher (59) m. Hopkins. He was an uncle of Rev. John Davenport (64). He was Mayor of Coventry, England 1602.

Issue of Henry Davenport (58), father of Rev. John Davenport, and his second wife, Elizabeth:

   I. Barnabus (60). He had two daughters and one son, Christopher, the famous Francis a' Santa Clara, the Franciscan.

  II. Edward (61).

 III. Christopher (62) Mayor of Coventry 1641.

 IV. Henry (63).

  V. Rev. John Davenport (64) b. 1597; went to America 1637.

NOTE:

Sir John Davenport, of the ninth generation, in Dr. Benedict Davenport's book on the Davenports, had issue.

(a) Thomas, (b) John, (c) Ralph, (d) Richard, (e) Roger, (f) Urian (the big man) (g) Arthur and (h) Margaret, who m. Sir John Hyde, Earl of Norbury. Their descendant, Edward Hyde, Earl of Clarendon, had dau. who m. James II of England, and they were the parents of Queen Mary, consort of King William, and of Queen Anne.

TOMBSTONE INSCRIPTIONS.

At Auvergne, Bourbon County, Kentucky (home of the late Hon. Brutus J. Clay, my grand-father.) His first wife's tomb bears this inscription:

(a)   "Amelia M. Clay
        Born Nov. 3, 1812
        Died July 31, 1943"
(Above copied by me May 5, 1940. H.B.D.)

At Edgehill Cemetery (Davenport Lot) Charles Town, W. Va., copied by me, July 26, 1931:

(b) Col. John T. Gibson, b. Jan. 3, 1825; d. Jan. 29, 1904.

(c) Mrs. Frances W. Gibson, b. Dec. 6, 1834; d. Oct. 21, 1909.

(d) Elizabeth B. Gibson, b. Nov. 3, 1858; d. June 25, 1895.

(e) Frances Williams, wife of Major Abraham Davenport, d. Sept. 17, 1829.

(f) William Davenport, b. Aug. 22, 1799; d. Apr. 19, 1815.

(g) Ariet Davenport, b. Aug. 22, 1795; d. 1803.

(h) Mrs. Rebecca Bryan, b. Apr. 8, 1793; d. July 5, 1816.

There are several other inscriptions which I did not copy.

Following are on Gibson lot.

(i) Margaret Holliday Gibson, b. Mar. 24, 1909; d. June 13, 1923.

Following notes not connected with above inscriptions.

Col. Ezekiel Field Clay, d. July 26, 1920. He was mother's brother.

Col. Braxton D. Gibson (my cousin) d. Aug. 14, 1946. aged ninety years, one day.

Benton Davenport, my son, d. May 1, 1938. He was b. Nov. 28, 1902.

Henry B. Davenport, III, my grandson, b. Feb. 28, 1936, at Charleston, W. Va.

(j) Sue Clay, b. Feb. 29, 1846; d. June 6, 1880.

(k) Brutus J. Clay, b. July 1, 1808; d. Oct. 11, 1878.

NOTE:

Sue Clay, above, was the first wife of Hon. Cassius M. Clay, II.

THE CLAY LINE.

The Davenport and Clay families were connected by the marriage on June 5th, 1860, of Henry B. Davenport (191) 1831-1901, of Altona, to Martha Irving Clay, daughter of Hon. Brutus Junius Clay and Amelia Field Clay, his wife, of Auvergne, Bourbon County, Ky.

THE CLAY FAMILY.

(Made partly from notes left by General Green Clay who died in 1828.)

(1) Sir John Clay of Wales married and had a son whose name was

(2) John Clay, and was known as Capt. Jno. Clay. He married in England and came to America on the ship Treasurer, in 1613. His wife, Anne, came over in 1624. He was living at Charles City, Virginia in 1624. He owned 1,200 acres of land. He had issue four sons, Francis, William, Thomas and Charles, of whom

(3) Charles Clay, son of Capt. John Clay, was born 1638 and died 1686. He married Hannah Wilson, daugh-

ter of John Wilson of Henrico Co., Va. He was a soldier in Bacon's rebellion, in 1676. He had a family of 7 children, among others Charles, Jr., who died in 1754, and who was the ancestor of Governor Clement Comer Clay of Alabama, and

(4) Henry Clay, son of Charles and Hannah Wilson Clay, was born 1672 and died 1760. He married Mary Mitchell of Chesterfield County, Va. She was born 1693 and died 1777. Henry Clay and Mary Mitchell Clay lived in Henrico Co., Va. They had issue six children ;among others, John Clay, died in 1761, the ancestor of Henry Clay of Ashland, and

(5) Charles Clay, born Jan. 31, 1716, died Feb. 25, 1789. He married Martha Green Nov. 11, 1741. She was born Nov. 25, 1719, died Sept. 6, 1793. She was a daughter of Thomas and Elizabeth (Marston) Green. He was born on the high seas, and was ever after called the "Sea Gull". Issue of Charles Clay (5) and Martha Green Clay were, among others, the following:

(6) Green Clay, known as General Green Clay, he having commanded the American Army at the battle of Fort Meigs. He was born Aug. 14, 1757, and died Oct. 21, 1828. Married March 14, 1795, Sally Lewis, daughter of Thomas and Elizabeth (Payne) Lewis. They had issue (among others) General Cassius Marcellus Clay, envoy to Russia, 1861-1869; he was born 1810, died 1905; and

(7) Brutus J. Clay, born July 1, 1808, died Oct. 12, 1878.

Married (1) Amelia Field, and (2) Anne Field. daughters of Col. Ezekiel Henry Field. Issue of Brutus J. Clay and Amelia Field (a) Martha Irvine, born Feb. 1, 1832, died May 28, 1908. Married Henry Bedinger Davenport. They had issue six children, viz, Junius Clay, Ezekiel Clay, Braxton (died an infant), Henry Bedinger, Amelia Field (who married Col. Catesby Woodford), and Braxton, who died unmarried at the age of 27.

(b) Christopher Field, born Nov. 20, 1835, married Mary Brooks, he died about 1899.

(c) Colonel Green Clay, born Feb. 11, 1839, died 1912, married Janie Rhodes.

(d) Ezekiel Field, born Dec. 1, 1840, died 1920 married (1) Mary L. Woodford and (2) Mrs. Florence Lockhart.

Issue of Brutus J. Clay and his second wife, Anne (Field) Clay:

(e) Hon. Cassius Marcellus Clay, born Mar. 26, 1846, died about 1913. He was married three times: (1) Sue Clay, (2) Pattie Lyman and (3) Mary Harris. He was president of the last Constitutional Convention of Kentucky.

Following are the lines of the several branches of the Clay Family:

Brutus J. Clay line	Henry Clay line
(1) Sir John Clay	(1) Sir John Clay
(2) Capt. John Clay	(2) Capt. Jno. Clay

(3) Charles Clay	(3) Charles Clay
(4) Henry Clay	(4) Henry Clay
(5) Charles Clay, Jr.	(5) John Clay
(6) Green Clay	(6) Rev. John Clay
(7) Brutus J. Clay	(7) Henry Clay, of
(8) Martha C. Davenport	Ashland
(9) Henry B. Davenport	(8) Col. Henry Clay
(10) Benton S. Davenport	(9) Anne Clay McDowell
(11) Henry B. Davenport,	(10) Judge Henry Clay
III	McDowell

Gov. C. C. Clay line

(1) Sir John Clay

(2) Capt. Jno. Clay

(3) Charles Clay

(4) Chas. Clay, Jr.

(5) William Clay

(6) Gov. Clement Comer Clay

(7) Sen. Clement C. Clay

(8) Line ran out, no children

From above chart it is seen that General Green Clay (6) was a grandson of Henry Clay (4) and that Rev. John Clay (6), the father of Henry Clay of Ashland, was also a grandson of Henry Clay (4). Hence General Green Clay (my great grandfather), was a first cousin of Rev. John Clay, the father of the statesman; also that General Green Clay and Governor Clement Clay were both great grandsons of Charles Clay (3). Brutus J. Clay (7) served in the Congress of the U. S., 1861-1865, and was chairman of the committee on agriculture. His son,

Colonel Green Clay was secretary of the American Embassy at St. Petersburg, Russia, 1861-1863, and from 1863-1869 was secretary of the American Embassy in Italy. He also served as a legislator in Mississippi and later as a state senator in Missouri.

ALABAMA LINE.

Gov. Clement Comer Clay (see above chart), son of William Clay and Rebecca (Comer) Clay, born, 1789 in Halifax Co., Va. Moved to Alabama in 1812, became Judge Circuit Court; Judge Supreme Court; Speaker of the House of Delegates; Member First Constitutional Convention of Alabama; Governor of the State; United States Senator; and was Commissioner to Digest the laws of Alabama. He died ____. His son Clement Claiborne Clay, born 1817, died 1882, was a member of the legislature; Judge of U. S. Court; U. S. Senator at age of 35, and while serving the second term in the Senate resigned to accept the Senatorship from Alabama in th Confederate States Senate at Richmond. His relative, A. S. Clay, became a United States Senator from Georgia.

Following is a more detailed statement of the General Green Clay line.

GENERAL GREEN CLAY LINE.

I. Green Clay, b. Aug. 14, 1757, d. Oct. 21, 1828. M. Mar. 14, 1795, Sally Lewis (b. 1776, d. 1867), daughter of Thomas Lewis, b. Mar. 8, 1749, and Elizabeth Payne, his wife. Issue of Green Clay and Sally Lewis:

(a) Elizabeth Lewis, who m. Col. John Speed Smith.

(b) Paulina, who m. Co. Wm. Rodes.

(c) Sally Ann, who m. (1) Col. E. Irvine, and (2) Hon. Madison C. Johnson. No issue.

(d) Sidney Payne.

(e) Brutus Junius (see below).

(f) Cassius Marcellus (see above).

(g) Sophia, died an infant.

II. Brutus Junius Clay, son of Gen. Green and Sally (Lewis) Clay, b. July 1, 1808, d. Oct. 12, 1878. M. Feb. 10, 1831, Amelia Field. She died July 31, 1843. He m. (2) Nov. 8, 1844, Anne Field, sister of his first wife. She was born Feb. 12, 1822 and died Apr. 16, 1881.

Issue (by first wife):

(a) Martha Clay, daughter of Brutus J. and Amelia (Field) Clay, b. Feb. 1, 1832, d. May 28, 1908. She married Jan. 5, 1860, Henry Bedinger Davenport, of Altona. For issue see below.

(b) Christopher (Kit) Field Clay, son of Brutus J. and Amelia (Field) Clay, b. Nov. 20, 1835, m. Mary Brooks. For issue see below.

(c) Green Clay, son of Brutus J. and Amelia Field Clay, b. Feb. 11, 1839, d. Nov., 1912. M. Janie Rhodes. For issue see below.

(d) Ezekiel Field Clay, son of Brutus J. and Amelia Field Clay, b. Dec. 1, 1840, d. July 20, 1920. Married (1) Mary L. Woodford, and (2) Mrs. Florence Lockhart. For issue see below.

Issue of Brutus J. Clay and Ann, his second wife:

(c) Cassius Marcellus Clay II, b. Mar. 26, 1846, d. ____.
M. (1) Sue Clay, (2) Pattie Lyman (3) **Mary Harris**. For issue see below.

III. Martha Clay Davenport, b. Feb. 1, 1832, m. Col.
Henry Bedinger Davenport, Jan. 5, 1860. She d.
May 28, 1908.
Issue:

(1) Junius Clay Davenport, b. Oct. 3, 1860; d. Feb.
1, 1945, m. Mary Trout. Issue: Junius Clay
Davenport, Jr. b. 1902.

(2) Annie Davenport, b. 12-11-05, m. John Franklyn
Newsom, 30 day of Oct., 1930.
Issue: Jack, born Feb. 24, 1936.
Mary, b. Dec. 6, 1938.

(b) Ezekiel Clay Davenport, b. Jan. 9, 1864, unmarried.

(c) Henry Bedinger Davenport, b. Feb. 11, 1865. M.
Dec. 24, 1893 (1) Emily McLane White, **daughter**
of Dr. I. C. White, and (2) Jan. 22, 1902, Alma F.
Stephenson, daughter of Thomas Benton Stephenson. She was born Aug. 19, 1881.
Issue:

(1) Benton Stephenson, b. Nov. 28, 1902, d. May 1, 1938
M. Imogene Coleman Mar. 17, 1933. Issue: Henry
B. Davenport III, b. Feb. 28, 1936.

(2) Braxton, b. Sept. 29, 1909, m. **Marjorie Chambers**,
Dec. 19, 1934.

(d) Amelia Field, b. Feb. 24, 1868, m. 1890, Col. Catesby Woodford, b. 1850, d. April, 1923. No issue.

(e) Braxton Davenport, b. Dec. 2, 1873, d. Oct. 13,
1900. Unmarried.

NOTES ON OTHER CHILDREN OF
BRUTUS J. CLAY.

Christopher (Kit) Field Clay, b. Nov. 20, 1835, died
about 1900. Married June, 1867, Mary F. Brooks of Bourbon Co., Ky.

Issue:

(a) Brutus J. Clay II, b. 1868, d. 1935.

(b) Samuel Brooks Clay, b. 1876, unmarried.

(c) Nannie Woodford Clay, b. 1874, d. June 15, 1893.

(d) Sadie Brooks Clay, b. 1876, d. June 13, 1893.

(e) Christopher Field Clay, Jr., b. _____. Accidentally
killed when about 23 yrs. old.

(f) Martha Davenport Clay, b. 1879, m. _____, Tom
Buckner. She d. 1937. Issue: daughter, Wornall b.
1916, m. (1)   (2) Eldon Hutchins 1938. Col. Green
Clay, b. Feb. 11, 1839, d. Nov. 1912. M. Janie Rhodes,
b. _____, d. _____.

Issue:

(a) Green Clay, b. 1872, d. 1896. M. Louise Campbell.
No issue.

(b) Rhodes Clay, b. 1874, killed in street duel in Mexico,
Mo. about 1909. Unmarried.

(c) Cassius Marcellus Clay, III, of Mexico, Mo., b. 1879
m. (1) Frances Cook (2) Bethel _____. No issue .

(d) Janie Clay, b. 1886, m. Col. Wm. Zeverly.
   Issue, a daughter, Janie, who m. (1) ____ Smith, and
   (2) _____.

   Col. Ezekiel Field Clay, b. Dec. 1, 1840, d. 1920, m. May
8, 1865, Mary L. Woodford, and (2) Mrs. Florence Lockhart. Issue of first marriage:

(a) Ezekiel Field Clay, Jr., b. June 16, 1871, d. Jan. 29,
   1915, m. (1) Anna C. Ward, b. 1870 d. 1900. (2) **Anne**
   Lee Washington, b. 1872, d. 1922. Issue first marriage:

(1) Carey Field Clay, b. 1900, d. 1946 m. Harriet Pooley.
   Issue 2 sons, (1) Sam Clay, (2) Carey Clay, Jr. **Lat-**
   ter died young.
   Issue second marriage:

   (1) Ezekiel Field Clay, III b. Jan. 4, 1910. m. **Grace J.**
   Arnold (2) Brent A. Clay b.   d.

(b) Woodford Clay, b. July 17, 1873, d. 1916, unmarried.

(c) Brutus Junius Clay, III. b. Nov. 28, 1876, d. Feb. 23,
   1926, m. Agnes McEvoy, of Baltimore, Md. Issue 6
   children, as follows:

(1) Mary, b. Dec. 3, 1913. Took the Veil.

(2) Annie, b. Nov. 18, 1915, m.   Keenan, of Atlanta,
   Ga. Issue:

(3) Brutus Junius, IV. b. Nov. 27, 1917, unmarried.

(4) Agnes,   b. July 3, 1919.

(5) Amelia Field,   b. Aug. 27, 1921.

(6) Catesby   b. July 25, 1923.

   NOTE: After the death of her husband, Brutus Junius Clay, III, his wife, Agnes McEvoy Clay, m. Hon.

Johnson M. Camden, former U. S. Senator from the State of Kentucky. His father, Hon. Johnson N. Camden, Sr., served two terms in the U. S. Senate from West Virginia.
(d) Buckner Clay, b. Dec. 30, 1877, d. Nov. 25, 1923, m. Juliet Staunton, of Charleston, W. Va. Issue: 2 sons.

   (1) Buckner Clay, Jr., and (2) Lyle Clay. After the death of her husband, Mrs. Juliet Staunton Clay m. Hon. Walter E. Clark, former Governor of Alaska.
(e) Amelia Field Clay, b. Feb. 15, 1880, m. Samuel Clay; he d. 1947. Issue:

   (1) James Clay, b. Nov. 3, 1912, m. 1947, Anne Ritter.
   (2) Mary Elizabeth Clay b. Aug. 28, 1915, m. 1947 Quentin Walker.
   (3) Samuel Clay, Jr. b. Apr. 11, 1917, m. Dorothy Lane.
(f) Mary Catesby Clay, b. June 17, 1883, d. Jan. 1944, m. C. Beverly Broun; issue, a daughter, Beverly Broun, b.
   Cassius Marcellus Clay, II., m. Mar. 26, 1946, d.   m.
   (1) Sue Clay, (2) Pattie Lyman, (3) Mary Harris. Issue of first marriage:
(1) Junius Brutus Clay, 3rd, b. Apr. 25, 1871, d.   m. Mary Hedges.
(2) Samuel Henry Clay, b. Apr. 7, 1873, died unmarried, Dec. 9, 1895.
(3) Anne Louise Clay, b. Sept. 22, 1877, m. Judge W. Rodes Shackleford, who d. 1935. Issue: 2 daughters:
   (1) Anne Field, m. Dr. Blanton 1937.

(2) ---------- m. ----------.

(4) Susan Elizabeth Clay, b. Apr. 3, 1880, m. Dr. Goodman, of British Army Medical Corps; lived in Cairo, Egypt many years.

Issue:

Issue of third marriage of Hon. Cassius Marcellus Clay (and Mary Harris):

(5) Cassius Marcellus Clay, 3rd, b. Mar. 2, 1895; m. (1) Emily Thomas.

Issue:

(a) Cassius m.   b. Nov. 29, 1923.

(b) Harris b. Dec. 27, 1926.

(c) Landon b. Mar. 12, 1926.

(2) Miram Berle

Issue:

(d) Mary Augusta b. Jan. 24, 1938.

(e) Rudolf Berle b. Sept. 10, 1939.

(6) John Harris Clay, b. Mar. 27, 1897, m. Dorothy Norton, of Louisville, Ky.

Issue:

(a) George Norton b. July 2, 1933.

(b) John Harris, b. Sept. 7, 1936.

(c) Mary Blythe m. Sept. 7, 1936—twins.

FIELD LINE.

(Numbers ( ) refer to number in Field Genealogy Book)

1. (30) William Field
2. (35) Richard Field will 1542.
3. (42) John Field astronomer 1525-1587.
4. (6762) John Jr. Field b. 1579. m. 1609

5. (5838¼) Henry Field b. 1611.
6. (6919) Abraham Field will 1674.
7. (6921) Abraham Jr., Field, d. 1775
8. (6927) Col. John Field killed at Point Pleasant battle Oct. 1774
9. (6955) Col. Ezekiel Henry Field, b. 1750, killed at Blue Licks 1782. Shawnee Indians captured him at Malden, Va., now W. Va.
10. (7005) Ezekiel Henry Field, Jr., b. 1782, m. Patsy Irvine.
11. (7070) Amelia Field, m. Brutus J. Clay, b. 1808, d. 1878.
12. (   ) Martha Clay, 1832-1908. m. Henry B. Davenport, 1831-1901
13.   Henry B. Davenport, Jr. b. 1865-
14.   Benton S. Davenport, 1902-1938
15.   Henry B. Davenport III, b. 1936-

THOMAS JEFFERSON (FIELD) LINE.

1. (30) William Field
2. (36) Rev. John Field, 1519-1587
3. (6761) Bishop Theopolis Field, 1574-1636
4. (6768) James Field, 1604
5. (6770) Major Peter Field, 1647-1707
6. (6772) Mary Field, 1679-1715. m. Capt. Tom Jefferson
7.   Peter Jefferson, 1708-1738, m. Randolph
8.   Thomas Jefferson, 1743-1826, President

Above chart shows relation of Davenport and Field families to Thos. Jefferson, 3rd President of U. S.

www.ingramcontent.com/pod-product-compliance
Lightning Source LLC
Chambersburg PA
CBHW080757300326
41914CB00055B/926